HE'S STILL SHOOTING

Joel D. Glover

He's Still Shooting

Copyright © 2024 Joel D. Glover

All rights reserved. No part of this book may be reproduced or transmitted in any form or by any means without written permission from the author.

ISBN: 978-0-9600469-6-6 (Paperback)
ISBN: 978-0-9600469-7-3 (ePub)
Also available for Kindle

Book design and layout: Lighthouse24

DEDICATION

With me being in the wildlife section, many in the enforcement section did not appreciate my law enforcement efforts. While enforcement was not my priority, I embraced it and worked hard to apprehend violators. My success was due to training from the officers in my county and my willingness to put forth the effort needed to make the apprehensions.

When the two veteran game wardens in our county retired, I took on a new role of training officer. It was a somewhat peculiar situation.

I quickly learned to embrace the role of teacher. I found myself understanding how my wife could enjoy being a classroom teacher for so many years. There is a lot of gratification in seeing a student grasp an idea or concept. There is a tremendous satisfaction when you see them put something you have taught them into practice. I have been fortunate to witness this many times. I have officers, who are now my supervisors, tell me that a wise man once told them...in reference to something I taught them. There is a lot of gratification in that.

In this book you will read about some of my efforts to train new officers. While I often referred to them as kids, that was not a jab at them, it was that when compared to me, most of them were kids. I'm sure the officers who trained me thought of me as a kid. Of course, I was a kid and they were ancient. Good grief, they were in their midforties!

What you are about to read is a mixed bag of tales from thirty-seven years of working as a certified wildlife biologist and conservation enforcement officer. In addition, you will hear about some traffic stops and Little League baseball. Just like my career, it's a mixed bag. However there has been one thing that has remained constant through the duration.

It's been a wild ride. Luckily, I wasn't in it alone. Through the hard times and through all the various coworkers there was one strong pillar that I leaned on. My wonderful wife was there supporting me 100 percent. I could not have asked for a better partner in life. I am so richly blessed to have her by my side, and I praise God for her each day. I dedicate this book to her. I love you, babe.

DISCLAIMER

The stories in this book are true to the best of my knowledge and recollection. I changed many of the names. I'm certain you will find some of these stories difficult to believe. As I've said before, I found them hard to believe, and I was there! These are my stories for your enjoyment. If you think you recognize someone in here, it's probably just your imagination.

CONTENTS

He's Still Shooting 1
Pots, Pans, and Panthers 11
You Can Ask Him! 16
You Don't Plant Scratch Feed 18
Rocket Science 24
She's Out! 29
Can I Have Your Autograph? 33
Night Hunting at the Chicken Houses 35
Blow in That Tube 39
Arrested for Carrying an Ink Pen 43
Fishing Forensics 50
This Is Your Lucky Day 54
Laser Surgery 57
The Biggest Turkey in the County 60
PETA Calling 68
Guilty as Charged 70
We're Not from Around Here 83
He Did What? 86
Rainbow People 97

Shots Fired—at Us!	101
Near Naked Pocket Baiter	108
Wait a Minute, Jack	111
Nobody Likes a Smart Aleck	116
Make Bag to Put Crap In	120
"OMG!"	124
Bird Psyche	129
Invisible Fence	132
How Big an Ole Boy Are You?	134
Deputy Dan	139
Trained Gator	144
Deficient Sample	147
Yellow Marshmallow People	151
Y'all's Sneaky	156
Traffic Court	159
Hunter Harassment	163
Got Any Prior Arrests?	168
Careful What You Ask For	174
Can't Catch Them All	176
Orange Hats on the Dash	180
Running When You Should Have Stayed	183
Hot Spot Biologist	186
Hope You Enjoyed It	190
Stolen Purse at Cedar Circle	194
Catch Him by Monday	196
Judges	201

Slow Learners with Short Memories	208
That Didn't Happen	210
Shhh!	215
280 Ballgame Traffic	218
Stargazers	224
Call the Police!	232
Shooting from the Porch	234
Hold Still	237
Epilogue	243

HE'S STILL SHOOTING

THE BEAM OF THE SPOTLIGHT illuminated the eyes of the deer. They shined brightly, like a piece of reflective tape on a thumb tack. There was a good reason for that. Suddenly, a shot split the night, then another and another. We were quickly barreling down the road toward the shooting when a fourth shot rang out. I loved it when a plan came together.

Don't ever let anyone tell you one person can't make a difference. In wildlife law enforcement a single tip followed up on can often lead to multiple arrests. Obviously, some tips are better than others, and over time a good conservation enforcement officer (CEO) learns to really appreciate an accurate tipster.

Someone who hasn't lived in a rural community may not understand the grapevine concept. Rural areas are much like a small town in that the residents have a way of knowing what's going on even in the absence of a local newspaper. Normally there will be one resident who is a mother lode of information. If that person is willing to share the info with you, it will go a long way toward increasing your effectiveness. If you want to keep the information flowing, you must follow up on each tip, make sure the tipster hears about the results (not always directly), keep their name out of it, and be sure to say thank you.

In the Marble Valley community of Coosa County, the man with his finger on the pulse of the area was a fellow we will call Chester. Chester was the constable, a civilian keeper of the peace, and was a former sheriff's deputy and investigator. Marble Valley is located in the far northwestern corner of the county and is most easily accessed by driving into adjacent Talladega County and curling back to it. It was definitely one of those "you can't get there from here" kind of places. Keep in mind that Coosa County was comprised of 652 square miles and had a population of less than eleven thousand people. Therefore, it probably goes without saying that Marble Valley was quite remote and sparsely populated and therefore was an excellent place for wildlife outlaws to practice their craft.

The residents of Marble Valley considered Chester to be "THE LAW" and called him with complaints and information. Being so far from the remainder of the county, response times for the sheriff's office or the game warden would be at least thirty minutes and sometimes much longer. Early in my career, CEO Hershel Patterson introduced me to Chester and told me when he called I needed to pay attention to what he had to say. I quickly found this to be true. I also soon learned Chester stood for what was right no matter who was involved. I learned this when I caught his son shooting the deer decoy from the road.

During the 2004–2005 deer season, Chester called me with a night-hunting complaint he said had occurred on Marble Valley Road near the clubhouse. The clubhouse was a landmark regularly used when giving directions in the valley. The details of this complaint were very similar to others we had been receiving from all over the county. The information was that the violator was hunting from his house. I believe this type of offense had increased in frequency due to several factors. One factor was the people were moving to where the deer lived. It would be very interesting to know how many night hunters had been caught in subdivisions that were new or still under construction. Of course, not all of these were residents, but several were. The deer eating the new grass in people's yards was just too much of a temptation for some people. In many areas the deer were moving to where the people lived. This was due to several factors, with an overpopulation of deer being chief among them. I remember one night when I returned to my home in Rockford, the county seat of Coosa County, and had twelve deer standing in my yard. It was not at all uncommon for me to hear deer crunching pecans in my side yard and have them within an arm's reach of my house. This was interesting in that my home was located maybe one hundred yards from the county courthouse! Another factor I feel influenced the increase in this violation was the fact that someone shooting from their house was pretty dang hard to catch. They have twenty-four hours a day they can decide to step outside or stick a gun out the window and shoot. The CEO is tasked with monitoring the entire county and can't spend every hour waiting on the outlaw to shoot from their house. It is often a frustrating situation.

Chester reported a fellow, whose name he wasn't sure of, had killed a ten-point buck at approximately eleven o'clock on Sunday night. He said the man had killed the deer across the road from his house while sitting on his front porch. I thanked him for the info and assured him I would check into it. Although at the time we had two CEOs in the county, neither one of them were familiar with Marble Valley and they had a combined total of three years of game and fish law enforcement experience. Things were about to change for them.

The next Sunday night found me hiding approximately five hundred yards from the suspect's house. My vantage point afforded a good view of the field in front of his home, but I could not see the house. At 9:30 p.m. a beam of light pierced the darkness and scanned the entire field. My heartbeat immediately accelerated as I anticipated a shot. The light was soon extinguished. I continued my vigil, and in about thirty minutes the field again was illuminated. Still, no shot. This pattern continued until almost midnight. At 12:30 a.m. I decided to take it in and began the long trek across the county.

The thirty-plus miles of crooked curving roads gave me a lot of time to mull over the situation. Shining across a public road was a violation; however, I did not want to settle for just a shining violation. As a matter of fact, the shining was actually a traffic law, and when we made the case, the fine went to the Department of Public Safety and we received seven dollars from the court costs!

This is probably a good place to straighten out a misconception. Many folks erroneously believe the conservation department, and for that matter police departments, are funded totally by money collected as fines and court costs. In the case of our department, fine monies consistently made up less than 2 percent of our budget. When people hear that, they often make an even more erroneous conclusion, assuming the conservation department is funded by their tax dollars. In most states that is not the case. The general public often doesn't know that conservation is primarily funded through the Wildlife Restoration Act, which has been in place since 1937. Each dollar the conservation department receives in license fees is matched with three dollars from the wildlife restoration monies. These monies are generated by excise taxes paid by sporting equipment manufacturers, which are in effect paid by hunters, fishermen, and recreational shooters. This is one of the few systems in the country where a group pays their own way without receiving tax dollars from the general fund. In Alabama, the Department of

Conservation receives no general fund monies. This fact often amazed citizens—and politicians, who felt certain they funded us.

Unlike most area wildlife biologists, I had an office outside of my home. Out of the goodness of my county forester's heart, I shared an office with the forestry commission. The morning after working the complaint, I was relating to my county forester, Blake Kelley, the events of the night before. When I told him where the property was and stated the fellow was shining the field across the road from his house, he commented the property there belonged to a local doctor. That revelation changed the whole complexion of the situation. I immediately began formulating a plan for the late-night shiner.

I almost immediately began trying to contact the doctor, which turned out to be quite a chore. Finally, in a weird twist of fate, I was able to contact the mother-in-law of the doctor. I introduced myself and explained the situation and she gave me a number where the doctor could be reached and I soon made contact. I gave him the details and asked for his assistance in rectifying the situation. He agreed to help and my plan was set.

While the job of wildlife biologist/CEO provided several perks, one of my favorites was the access to doctors. I'm not speaking about the ability to get in and see a doctor, but rather the ability to get a doctor on the phone. Many times, I called a doctor's office and told the receptionist I needed to speak to the doctor only to hear the disdain in their voice as they explained the doctor was not available. I would then advise them I was the wildlife biologist or CEO working on the doctor's property and there would immediately be a marked change in their demeanor as they now politely asked me to hold and the doctor would quickly be on the line. I loved that!

I contacted my two county officers and we rode over to check the area out. Chester had mentioned the suspect had a golf-putting green across the road from his house and he thought that was where the ten-point had been killed. We were soon in the area and rolled past the location. Sure enough, about fifty yards off of the road was a "golf green" approximately four hundred square feet in size, complete with a flag marking the hole. However, the green wasn't entirely green. In fact, it was more yellow than green. Although it was winter, the yellow spots were not dead grass, they were piles of corn! The number of charges were really beginning to add up, if only we could catch him in the act of shooting. With the landowner's help, I had a plan for that.

Tuesday night found me and my two partners standing at my hiding spot down the road from the violator's house. We were about to embark on a very dangerous detail, one not exactly like any I had ever tried. We had conferred about the situation and agreed we didn't have much unless the fellow actually shot. For that reason, we were now walking through the tall grass of the field in front of the violator's house carrying, as safely as possible, a deer decoy! One officer carried the body, the other carried the head, and I carried the antlers and reflective eyes. We knew how risky this was; yet we were confident this plan would work.

Things were working well right up until the spotlight came on. I must admit the wisdom of this decision was somewhat in question as the three of us hugged the ground as the light scanned above us. The light soon went out and we were up and moving again. For safety's sake we were making a wide arc around the field, taking advantage of a depression that provided cover. We were soon directly in front of the violator's house and we were moving up toward the corn-covered golfing green when once again the spotlight illuminated the area. As we laid on the ground with the light sweeping over us, we made final plans. As soon as the light went off, we ran to the green and stood the deer up in the corn. I attached the head with the antlers and reflective eyes and turned on the power, and we all three ran toward the truck.

Our predetermined plan was for one officer to hide in the field about one hundred yards from the deer and the house so he could observe what went on firsthand while the other officer and I waited at the truck, ready to move in and make the apprehension we were hopeful would occur quickly. We were soon back at the truck, where we crossed our fingers and began our wait.

Working night hunting can be the most boring or the most exciting pursuit in wildlife law enforcement. There are often many long hours spent sitting in the middle of nowhere with absolutely nothing going on. I have logged many hours watching a field or roadside without one vehicle passing my vantage point all night long. It is definitely a hit-or-miss proposition. However, the monotony can change to total exhilaration in mere seconds. This night our wait was a short one.

We had been at the truck less than five minutes when we saw the field light up. We immediately jumped in the truck and tried to control the rush of adrenaline that coursed through our veins. Almost as quickly as it had come on, the light went off. This was puzzling, but before I had time to try to decipher what was going on, the light was back on. Then it went off. We waited for maybe ten seconds and the light came back on and then a thunderous blast split the still night. I started the truck and we were quickly flying down the road toward the source of the shot. Quickly another shot rang out and then another. As the house came into view, a fourth shot sounded and my partner, Shannon, yelled, "He's still shooting!" This exclamation was not to inform me of what was happening but was to say, hey, you are driving me directly into the line of fire, which I was! I had all fourteen, yes fourteen, of my blue-and-clear strobe lights flashing as we slid into the driveway. As I observed the man ducking into the house, rifle in hand, I knew things had just been escalated a few notches.

One of several problems associated with attempting to apprehend someone hunting from their house is they can take refuge in the house. This presents a much different dynamic than we are used to dealing with. Someone hiding in their own home is much more difficult to apprehend than someone in a vehicle. However, on the other hand, one small advantage is you normally know who you are after when they are hunting from their house. Such was the case this night and I immediately got on the public address system in my truck and called the man's name and ordered him out of the house. After not receiving any reaction, I called the sheriff's office and told them what was going on and asked that they get me the phone number for the house. I again ordered the man out of the house over the truck's loudspeaker.

In a few seconds I spotted movement at the rear of the house as the man came into view. To say we were on high alert would be a great understatement. I yelled at the man to raise his hands and he put them up at about shoulder height. Although this revealed he no longer had the rifle, I yelled "All the way up!" and he complied. I gave him the loud verbal command to walk toward me and he responded, "I don't have any shoes on," to which I responded, "That sounds like a personal problem. Walk!" I shouted, and he began walking toward me. I instructed him to turn around and get down on his knees. As he complied, CEO Shannon Calfee moved in and applied the handcuffs.

We were still operating on adrenaline when I asked, "What on earth do you think you are doing?" To this the man responded, "I've got a coyote problem. They killed my dog and I'm trying to protect my family." "Was that what you shot at?" I asked, and he replied, "Yes, two of them ran across my trail." I told Shannon to start writing the tickets and I eased down to the field and retrieved the decoy. I came back and placed the deer in the back of my truck without the defendant seeing me. I came around to the subject and told him, "You are an unlucky fellow." "Why?" was his belligerent reply. I informed him, "The coyotes you shot at must have run right in front of a deer because you hit it in the shoulder four times! Either that or you're just a liar!" I received a nasty sneer and I said, "Let's take him to jail."

After receiving permission from the defendant's wife, we had entered the house and retrieved the rifle from the two-year-old daughter's closet. We also acquired a handheld spotlight. While we were finishing the tickets, I got to thinking this guy had probably not been able to hold the light and repeatedly fire the rifle. I pulled the officers aside and asked what they thought. Both agreed he had probably had some assistance.

I went to the porch and summoned the wife to the door. I advised her of her rights and asked her to tell me what had occurred. She stated they just liked to look at the deer. I told her they had done more than look tonight. She again said they just liked to look at the deer. I could tell we were getting nowhere fast so I decided to try another track. I asked, "If you and your husband both go to jail tonight is there anyone who can come and get your children?" "He did it" was her immediate reply. "He said something about an eight point and he grabbed the rifle." I asked who held the light and she said, "I held it." We began filling out her tickets.

We decided we would charge the shooter with hunting at night, shooting across a public road, hunting without a permit, and hunting by the aid of bait. In Alabama, the definition of hunting includes anyone giving assistance to someone hunting. Therefore, the wife received all of the same charges.

The pair appeared in court the next month. The wife was called first and immediately pled guilty to all charges. The husband also pled guilty. The judge accepted their pleas and fined the pair $5,842, suspended their hunting privileges for three years, and sentenced them to 360 days in jail, which he suspended on the payment of the fine, which they paid immediately.

Two game wardens who had been working less than two years and a wildlife biologist/game warden made a case unlike any they would probably ever make again. It was an extremely dangerous undertaking and I was elated that we were able to pull it off. I think it made a really good story. I hope you think so too!

POTS, PANS, AND PANTHERS

ONE OF THE GREATEST BANES of wildlife biologists in the Southeast is the myriad reports of the elusive black panther. Once again, if I had a dollar for every report of a big cat I received it would very nicely supplement my retirement. Let me tell you right up front there has never been a documented case of a black or melanistic panther anywhere in North America. Believe me when I tell you making such a statement in many of the surroundings I found myself in wasn't good for my health. I have had many folks become fighting mad when I told them I was sure they had seen something but I was even more sure it wasn't a black panther. They did not want to hear that.

I remember well during the first year of my career I was invited to give a talk at the Marble Valley Community Club in the far northwest corner of Coosa County. I prepared a very informative talk on the wild turkey. I had been able to assist on the Tallahala turkey project in south Mississippi as a Mississippi State University graduate student. The Tallahala project was a landmark research effort on turkeys in the Southeast and therefore I had a lot of good info to disseminate. I arrived at the clubhouse, a small white building on the side of the road in the middle of nowhere, and set up my projector and slides. This was before PowerPoint was ever thought of. I was briefly introduced by Conservation Enforcement Officer (CEO) Hershel Patterson and launched right into the talk. After about forty-five minutes of thrilling slides, commentary, and anecdotes that provided an in-depth look into the life and times of the wild turkey, I finished and asked if the group had any questions. I felt I had covered the topic well and was ready for almost anything they wanted to know. Oh, to be young and naive. An old man, probably like forty-five or so, which seemed old then, wearing a plaid shirt and blue jeans raised his hand. I did not know whether he was a turkey hunter, landowner, or maybe both, but it really didn't matter; I was anxious to hear his question. I acknowledged the man and he posed his question to me. "What about the black panthers we have around here?" I had not seen that curve ball coming. It was as if I had been kicked in the stomach! I was not sure exactly what to say, which was likely evident by my stammering around. Finally, I gathered my courage and shakily stated, "There is no such thing as a black panther." Talk about making a good impression! As soon as the words left my mouth an audible gasp emanated from the room. The thought of pulling my backup pistol out and shooting myself in the leg quickly crossed my mind. I looked at Hershel and saw he was wearing a look that said, "You've got to handle it." The questioner merely scoffed at my answer and gave me a "You're just another government biologist" look. I asked if there were any more turkey questions. Hearing none, I wrapped things up.

Although this was my first encounter with those who believed in the existence of black panthers, it would definitely not be my last. I would soon learn many folks are obsessed with seeing a black panther. You would not believe the number of reports I received concerning the big cats.

When my best student, Jerry Fincher, began work as the CEO in Talladega County, it didn't take long for him to get his initiation into black pantherdom. It just so happened I was with him when he received a call from the Talladega Police Department telling him they were in pursuit of a black panther. It seemed the town animal control officer had somehow happened upon the big, black cat and had taken a shot at the beast. Although not positive, the officer felt certain he had hit the cat and would have it soon. Jerry looked at me and said he guessed he had better head that way. I told him I wouldn't be in too big of a hurry. We had already had a discussion about the panthers and I reminded him I didn't know what they had seen but if it was a black panther it would be the first one ever. However, I warned him to be careful when telling folks there were no black panthers. We parted and he headed toward the call.

As it turned out the calls kept coming for the next two days. On the third day I radioed Jerry and asked him the status of the cat. He informed me he had received a call at two o'clock in the morning telling him they had the monster cornered under a house. I knew his patience was wearing thin when he told me he responded to the caller with, "Tell them to kill it and call me when they have it dead!" When I asked if he had received another call his simple reply was, "Nope."

I once received a call from my supervisor, Rick Claybrook, stating there had been a report of a big cat in northern Elmore County and he wanted me to go and check on it. As it turned out, I was tied up on something I couldn't get out of so Rick told me he would handle the call. Bless his heart. Rick was a good supervisor in that he wouldn't ask you to do anything he wouldn't do himself. However, after he gave me a report on what he had found, I sort of hate I missed it.

Rick said when he arrived the first thing he noticed was the yard was littered with pots and pans. The cookware was not randomly strewn in the yard; every pot and pan appeared to have been placed open side down. He made his way to the door where he was met by the homeowner, who was really excited to see him. He described the man as small in stature and very nervous. The man told him he was very worried about the big cat he had heard scream repeatedly. When he noticed Rick was looking at all the pots and pans, he told him each one was covering a track he wanted Rick to identify.

The two moved to the first pot. Rick said the man reached down and grasped the pot with both hands and quickly jerked it off the ground. Rick said he couldn't help but jump back a little since the fellow acted as if something was surely going to come running out. He said the man picked up every pot and pan in the same snatching manner, and every time Rick told him the track was a dog track. After lifting the last pot and getting the same response the man dropped his head and sighed. He then came forth with an admission. "Well, that makes sense. Last night I heard that cat scream out and I came out on the porch with my gun and saw something running across the yard." The man hesitated and then admitted, "I shot and I killed my dog." Rick said his first impulse was unbelief, followed by the urge to laugh. However, he regained his composure and told the homeowner he hated to hear that. He listened as the homeowner told him how good the dog was and he sure hated he had shot him by mistake but he just couldn't take a chance on the big cat coming in his yard. Rick left after telling the man to call again if he had any more trouble. Evidently after the man had shot his dog, the big cat knew he meant business and found another neighbor to terrorize, seeing how we didn't receive another call.

The question of the black panther was never ending. In addition, I received just as many calls concerning brown big cats. Although I felt the majority of these calls were unfounded, I can't say that for all of them. In addition, as I progressed through my career I learned people would keep any- and everything as a "pet." The "pet" list was long and included bears, black mamba snakes, raccoons, mountain lions, and everything in between. Therefore, I always tried to tell folks I would try not to doubt anything they saw because somebody down the street may have just released it.

I truly believe many of the people who reported the panthers really had seen something. I also believe many folks wanted to see a panther so badly they convinced themselves they had seen one. The mind can definitely play tricks on you. Our officers in Elmore County once responded to the call of a dead bear. It turned out to be a mule!

While I never saw a black panther, I did see a black panther crossing, or at least a black panther crossing sign. While hosting a landowner tour in Coosa County on the Bill Dark property, I rounded a curve in the road and found someone had erected a large yellow traffic sign with a black panther on it. Of course, I immediately knew my friend and colleague Ricky Porch, the president of the local Panther Paw Pals (a panther believers' group) had been hard at work! That was a good one, Ricky.

YOU CAN ASK HIM!

WE'VE ALL HEARD THE PHRASE about best laid plans. It sure is irritating when something you have carefully planned for and anxiously awaited gets messed up by some obviously unlearned individual. But when it happens twice, that's beyond the pale.

Opening day of the Alabama deer season is circled on a lot of calendars. Although our season now lasts for almost four months, avid hunters can't wait for the season to arrive. There is a lot of preparation necessary in readying your equipment, preparing habitat, and erecting or checking existing stands. All of these activities help build the anticipation of opening day. After all of the preparation, folks don't appreciate somebody messing things up. That includes not only the game warden but other folks as well.

The landowner walked briskly through the cold morning air en route to his tree stand. It was opening day of the Alabama gun deer season. The man had looked forward to this morning since the season had ended nine months earlier. Arriving at the tree, he encountered one of the most frustrating occurrences in the deer woods. Looking up in his tree stand he observed a camo-clad man perched there. In no uncertain terms he ordered the poacher out of the stand. Once on the ground, the landowner delivered a severe tongue-lashing, explaining he did not put forth the time, expense, and effort of putting up the stand to have some poacher use it. He ended the tirade with, "Don't you ever come back on this property."

With his hunt ruined, the aggravated landowner returned home. The next morning, the hunter once again made his way to his stand. The landowner could not believe his eyes when he reached his destination and found the stand once again occupied by the same scoundrel. Obviously, the stern warning had fallen on deaf ears. This time the landowner was ready to take some action. Not sure where to go, he drove to the county sheriff's office.

Had he been a few years younger the crusty old landowner would have likely dealt with things in a different manner. However, at seventy years old, he felt it best to let the authorities handle things. While he didn't like to see folks get in trouble, he had given a clear and concise warning the previous day that had not been taken seriously.

The deputy at the sheriff's office curiously eyed the old man dressed in blue denim overalls and a brown Carhartt coat with a faded orange cap on his head and a disgusted look on his face. There was no mistaking his outrage as the landowner began telling the deputy the situation of how for two days in a row a poacher had been in his deer stand on his property and finished the tirade by saying he wanted something done about it! The deputy stated he could see how that would be upsetting and agreed something needed to be done. He asked the landowner if he had been able to get the poacher's name. The man replied, "No, but come on outside and I'll open the trunk and you can ask him!"

You can't make this stuff up!

YOU DON'T PLANT SCRATCH FEED

FOR MANY YEARS opening day of dove season was one of the busiest days of the year for conservation enforcement officers (CEOs). I feel safe to say more licenses were checked on that day than on any other. Many folks who didn't hunt anything else would shoot doves on opening day. It was very much a social event and things usually went well until the game warden showed up. Nothing ruined a good dove shoot like "the man" walking onto the field!

A county that was 92 percent forested did not offer a lot of mourning dove habitat. Doves are seed eaters and are not good scratchers. They normally feed in weed fields and harvested crop fields. While we had a few weed fields and several wildlife openings, we were lacking when it came to crop fields. We had little or no commercial agriculture. There were a couple of truck farmers in the county. These were folks who primarily grew vegetables and either sold them out of their truck or to local grocery stores. These "farms" were small and provided little food that a dove could utilize. This being the case, when we did have someone shooting doves in our county, we knew the area needed to checked to make sure it was on the up-and-up.

Whether or not a dove field was legal was often the source of bitter debate. Evidently the definition of what was legal was difficult for many to understand. It was perfectly legal to manipulate a standing crop to make it more attractive to doves. For example, if you had grown a field of corn, grain sorghum, sunflowers, or millet you were allowed to mow it, burn it, or even feed it in a shredder and blow it out onto the field. You could not remove anything from the field and bring it back later, although this was often attempted.

In addition to manipulating a standing crop you could hunt over a planted field provided it was a "normal agricultural practice." What constituted a normal practice was yet another subject of debate. Obviously, there were multiple legal ways to have a good dove shoot. The problem was that preparing a legal dove field meant someone was going to have to put forth a lot of effort over a considerable period of time.

Creating a legal field that would produce seeds attractive to doves took some planning. Since our dove season normally opened on the second Saturday of September, it was imperative that planted crops would mature a couple of weeks prior to opening day in order to give the birds time to find the seed. Seeing how seed-producing species commonly planted for doves, such as millet or grain sorghum, normally require eighty to ninety days to mature, these plantings needed to take place in late May or early June. This would entail preparing a good seedbed and planting and covering the seed. Once the crop matured, it was often necessary to either cut it for hay, burn it, or mow it in order to scatter the seed, making it available to doves. This required multiple trips to the field and a considerable amount of time. With this being the case, many found it was a lot easier to go out a couple of weeks prior to the season and broadcast some cracked corn or rock salt and have a lot of birds on opening day. Many would go as far as rolling out sheets of plastic in an open field and spreading the bait on the plastic. On the day before the hunt they would simply roll up the plastic containing any remaining bait and remove it from the field. That way the next day the birds would come to the field looking for the seed but when we came there would be nothing illegal there. A lot of folks put forth as much effort to do it wrong as it would have taken to do it right! Others would try to do things right, but just couldn't get a handle on what could be done. I met one such fellow on a hot opening day in September.

While checking a dove shoot on the east side of Coosa County, we could hear occasional shots indicating another nearby shoot. Based on the shots, it sounded like maybe four or five shooters were on the field. We concluded our current business and made our way to the next field.

When arriving at a field where shooting is taking place there are several things that a CEO needs to do. If possible, before you enter the field, you need to determine how many shooters you have and their locations. This can be difficult since all of the folks will be wearing camouflage and will likely be hidden in the shade somewhere around the field. If there aren't many birds flying and consequently little shooting, it can be difficult to locate folks. It's a good idea to try to watch the field from a concealed location prior to making your presence known; however, that often isn't possible.

When you enter the dove field you always have to be on your toes. You may have people run from you or run to you. There may be someone who begins throwing doves into the woods or weeds to make sure they are below the fifteen-bird limit by the time you get to them. Someone may be frantically breaking down their shotgun and inserting a dog fennel stalk to act as a "plug" so their gun will not hold more than three shells, which is the legal limit when hunting migratory birds. There are many things to watch for and this is why it is a good idea to have multiple officers if possible.

Briefly surveying this "field" from cover revealed it was a small shoot with five hunters shooting over a small pasture area. The fact doves were flying into a pasture made things suspect from the get-go. Closer inspection revealed a disk had been pulled through the pasture but to say it was disked was a major stretch. After gathering the hunters and checking their licenses, I took a closer look at the "field." It was obvious the area had been "planted" but I did find a major problem. As I examined the ground I found grain sorghum, cracked corn, and other bits and pieces of various seeds. I asked who had prepared the field and a man stepped forward and informed me it was his field. I told the man the area was baited and he immediately, belligerently responded, "No it's not!" Although I understood the man didn't want the field to be baited, I also understood I would be the one making that call.

The defiant man was obviously upset we had checked his shoot and was now really upset I had declared his shoot was illegal. While I understand someone not agreeing with my assessment, I could see this fellow was quickly getting a little too worked up. Experience had taught me someone getting all worked up could easily make some bad decisions so I kept a close eye on the fellow.

Although not unusual, it was interesting that the other four people had not uttered a single word. The spokesman launched into his explanation stating he had watched a local TV hunting show and the host had said if you disked a field and planted it, you could legally hunt over it. I countered that was true to an extent but it was evident he had not followed those instructions. You would have thought I had slapped the man in the face. The way he was huffing and puffing and stomping around, I was glad I had unloaded his shotgun.

I attempted to explain that while it was debatable whether or not he had a well-prepared seedbed, that wasn't his largest problem. I was beginning to be able to check the man's pulse rate by watching the vein on the side of his forehead! I explained his biggest problem was he had not planted seed; he had "planted" scratch feed. Scratch feed was normally comprised of a blend of cracked corn and small grains commonly fed as a supplement to chickens and domestic ducks, geese, and turkeys. While it was technically made up of seeds, broadcasting it on a poorly prepared seedbed definitely did not constitute a bona fide agricultural practice.

The man stood looking at me with his mouth hanging open. As I retrieved my ticket book and asked for everyone's driver's license, the man asked if we could talk. We stepped away from the group.

You never knew what might be coming during a "private" conversation. Sometimes it was a confession they did not want others to hear and other times it was their attempt to get out of the situation by telling you who they were or who they knew.

This fellow had evidently decided the belligerent route would not work and was now much more conciliatory as he explained the others on the field were his boss and coworkers from Georgia and seeing how he had invited them this was not going to bode well for him. I explained it was a little worse than he knew. This time he looked at me with a pitiful look like he was about to throw up. I informed him since the others were from out of state, we would probably have to take them to jail. Although it was a hot day with the sun beating down, this fellows face was white as a sheet. I literally thought he was going to be physically sick and stepped back to give him room in case he began to hurl. It would not be the first time that had happened!

The fellow who had been a defiant dove field authority had now morphed into a sniveling beggar. "Please don't take them to jail. If you do I will surely lose my job!" I realized this guy was in a bad situation. Due to the hot weather and my ample girth I was sweating profusely but nothing like this guy! I was afraid he might dehydrate right in front of me. I think if he could have disintegrated on the spot he would have.

I considered our options and came up with a plan. I explained since the folks had purchased their nonresident licenses and since I believed he had made a genuine effort to prepare a legal field (although he had fallen way short) and since dove hunting by the aid of bait carried a low fine, I would allow him to sign a hefty bond that would likely cover the fines and costs of everyone involved. This was before we became a participant in the Violator Compact, which would allow us to have folks in other states picked up on our charges. He jumped at the chance to sign the bonds. In fact, I think he would have signed anything at that point! I thoroughly explained that by signing the bonds for everyone involved it would be his responsibility to see that each defendant either appeared in court or paid their fine and costs prior to court. If that did not occur, the bonds would be forfeited and he would have to pay the bond amount. He assured me he would pay the fines and costs personally. The man thanked me profusely.

With the paperwork and explanations complete, we moved on to the next field. I could be wrong, but I would bet it will be an ice-cold day in September before that guy will ever host another dove shoot.

Because the guy in this story felt he was responsible for the situation, he paid the price for the whole group. That's admirable. What if he had not been guilty at all? Do you think he would have done that? Probably not. However, that has happened. Jesus lived a sinless life here on earth and yet died on a cruel cross to atone for your sins and mine. Jesus offers us forgiveness of sin and eternal life. If you haven't already accepted the offer, do it today. There is no one else who can take your place or make your choice!

ROCKET SCIENCE
(DETERMINED TO HUNT OVER BAIT)

FOR THE FIRST THIRTY-TWO YEARS of my career I spent a lot of time looking for baited areas and attempting to catch people hunting deer by the aid of bait. In large part that came to an end when the legislature passed a law establishing a bait license which allowed folks to hunt deer by the aid of bait.

I must admit I was very much opposed to the legalization of bait on several fronts. First, I believe it is less than a fair chase to sit over a pile of corn and shoot the deer that are attracted to it. Furthermore, as a wildlife biologist, I knew anytime you place animals in close proximity to one another the chance of disease transmission is increased. Possibly what bothered me the most was the fact the baiting would no doubt result in a huge amount of corn being dumped in the woods and fields. Much of that corn would be of low quality and would contain aflatoxins that are detrimental to many species but especially to turkeys. Turkeys have a hard enough time trying to survive without adding disease into the mix. Lastly, I could not see how the addition of the bait to the landscape would not strengthen predator numbers and boost the wild hog populations that were already destroying the habitat of most species. Did I mention I was against it?

Back in the good ole days when we regularly worked bait, the elements of a baiting case were basically always the same.

However, the cases and the time it took to make a bait case varied widely. While some cases were made the first time you checked a property, others could literally take years to apprehend the violator. Literally years! Every time you checked a baited area you ran the risk of being spotted either by the violator or by someone who would tell the violator or by getting your picture on a game camera. Today it seems there is a camera hung on every other tree in the woods! For this reason, working bait often encompassed a lot of walking after parking in a remote location. However, there were also cases where you could literally check the bait while driving by in a vehicle.

After the two veteran game wardens in Coosa County retired it seemed as though the new officers came and went as through a revolving door. I enjoyed working with them since they usually came in without the preconceived notion that conservation enforcement officers (CEOs) shouldn't work with wildlife biologists. Unfortunately, it didn't take long for other officers to share their bias with these officers. However, the officers were normally sharp enough to understand whether or not I knew what I was doing. The fact I led the state in the number of arrests by wildlife biologists for the majority of my career should have given the other CEOs a heads-up.

One of our young CEOs, who I'll call Bud, and I had located some bait on a property in the south part of Coosa County. On our first day checking the bait we apprehended one individual who explained he hadn't put the bait out but knew it was there. This of course prompted us to ask who else was hunting the area. The man gave us the names and the type of vehicles the others would be driving. Now you are probably wondering what good it would do us to know the others in the club since we had caught one member and he would surely tell the others. Well you would be surprised how many times we made multiple arrests on the same property without one member telling the other they had been caught. Many folks seemed to have the mindset that if getting in trouble was good enough for them it was good enough for everybody.

After our initial catch, we had monitored the property regularly. Finally, on a Saturday afternoon we passed by the clubhouse and saw the vehicle we had been told belonged to the one who had put out the bait. I suggested to Bud we wait until about 3:00 p.m. to come back and check the bait. Seeing how it was getting dark around five o'clock we agreed the suspected violator would be in the woods by then. We checked a couple of other areas and pulled up at Wayside Church to wait for 3:00 p.m. to arrive. Wayside Church was approximately one-half mile from the Elmore County line in the far south end of the county. It was about two miles from the baited area.

It's always interesting how time flies until you are watching the clock. Then it just drags along. The digital clock clicked over to 3:00 and I said to Bud, "Let's go get him."

Feeding had been taking place directly under the stand and there was also a feeder hanging in a tree about one hundred yards from the tree stand. It was somewhat of a unique setup in that a field road led literally to the base of the ladder stand. The baited area was about three hundred yards from the camp house. We were confident the fellow would be in the stand as we neared the camp house. However, you never knew what might happen when working bait.

Our high hopes were dashed on the rocks as we passed the camp house and there walking down the side of the county road with his rifle slung over his shoulder was our hunter. "Dang!" Bud exclaimed as he slammed on the brakes. "Go, go, go," I said as we were too close to get stopped. Bud accelerated and we blew by the guy.

"Well, that's that," the dejected game warden said.

"Maybe not," I replied.

"Well I can tell you if the game warden drove by me on my way to a baited stand there is no way I'd go and get in it!"

I agreed that most people wouldn't; however, I reminded Bud we rarely dealt with rocket scientists in our line of work and maybe this guy wouldn't pay us any attention. I told Bud to pull over at Shady Grove Church and we would give it until 3:30 or so and try it again. I don't know if you've noticed, but churches played a major role in my career. I can't tell you how many times we used a church parking lot to meet or we hid behind a church or in a cemetery while working night hunting. Thankfully each community in the county had multiple churches, which worked well for us.

As we sat watching the clock, Bud continued to lament about our bad luck and how he knew the fellow wouldn't be there. The officer had good reason to be upset. Of all the guys I had ever worked bait with, Bud had the worst luck of them all. He had been busted checking baited areas more times than either of us wanted to recall and we were both afraid we were about to add another incidence to that list. Getting caught attempting to locate or working bait was frustrating to say the least. That was especially true when you had spent hours, days, or even a whole season attempting to apprehend the violator.

At 3:30 we headed back to the area. We pulled off onto the woods road and I noted the feeder was still hanging in the tree. Bud was still saying the guy would not be in the tree as we drove directly under the man sitting in the stand, rifle in hand. "I can't believe it!" was all the shocked officer could utter. We called the fellow down and wrote him a citation for hunting by the aid of bait.

I must admit I had doubts about whether or not the guy would be in the tree and I was thankful he was. While completing the arrest paperwork, Bud asked the man where he was employed and we were both surprised when he replied, "NASA." Bud finished the paperwork and we returned to our truck. As we headed toward Rockford I had to eat my words as I told Bud maybe his bait luck was changing seeing how it wasn't every day we caught a rocket scientist!

SHE'S OUT!

I THOUGHT I WOULD GIVE you a break from game warden stories at least for a minute. I've told many folks that I was a Little League umpire for fifteen years but I had to give it up and get into something less dangerous like chasing armed criminals through the dark in the middle of the night! And you thought the game warden stories were scary!

Working as a Little League umpire was an eye-opening experience. Believe me when I tell you umpires don't win any popularity contests. A line I often used in umpiring was, "I've been called worse than that by better people than you."

One thing many parents and fans evidently don't understand is the umpire is the supreme authority on the ball field. What he or she says is the way it is. Sure, you can protest the game and you might win, but that happens about as often as a triple play.

Umpires have been scrutinized probably since the first game and have normally been found to be pretty good. Of course, there is your occasional bad apple, but that's always true, and even if he is blind, his calls on the field stand.

In my experience, I rarely had any trouble with players. I made it clear I didn't need a ten- or twelve-year-old questioning my call and they rarely did. The coaches and parents were a whole different ball game. I would do my best to listen to an argument posed in a respectful manner, but I didn't need to have somebody yelling at me. That was especially true when they didn't know what they were talking about.

I admit an umpire missing a call is aggravating. I have observed umpires missing calls and it is frustrating. However, in my experience someone going ballistic normally doesn't get things straightened out.

I was calling a girls' softball game, not my favorite situation, when a line drive hit a home team base runner standing on third base. I immediately called the base runner out and the crowd erupted. It seemed everyone in the stands was screaming as if they had just been gutted with a dull butter knife. The ringleader was a fellow whose daughter was a pretty good athlete and was on the team. He fashioned himself as being very knowledgeable about the game and I knew he thought of me as being just the opposite. His daughter was a pitcher and every time I failed to call her high pitches a strike he would yell out, "That was a rise ball," meaning I didn't realize it was reaching the mitt high but was coming through the zone. Although I usually just ignored him, occasionally I would respond it must have risen too much. I digress. After I called the base runner out, he was up out of his seat and yelling that the girl who had been hit with the line drive was on the base when the ball hit her.

Unfortunately, many parents and fans never move beyond the rules normally used in the backyard. In Little League baseball and softball, the base is not a sanctuary. The bases are located within the field of play. The rules state if a base runner is struck by a batted ball before the ball has passed an infielder, the runner is out. This rule is in place because the ball being deflected by a base runner could give the offense an unfair advantage. It was very obvious a lot of the ball fans present didn't know this was the rule.

The uproar over the call was not subsiding. Not only were they yelling at me, they were also yelling at the coach and demanding that he do something.

Although I knew better, I could not resist. I went to the fence and looked right at the man and asked, "Was she on the base?" He looked at me and gave an emphatic "Yes." I replied, "Then she's out," using my best fist pump for emphasis!

It wasn't the professional way to handle things, but I must admit, I did feel pretty good about it. Of course, the coach wanted to see it in the rule book and although umpires aren't required to honor such requests, I showed it to him. He turned to the crowd and reluctantly told them I was correct and the game continued.

Yelling at the umpire reflects the attitude of our culture today when it comes to authority. I'm sure I don't have to tell you, folks today resist any type of authority. There is a real problem with that. What disturbed me the most while officiating baseball was the parents or coaches who told players what had happened was the umpire's fault. When the athletes realize their coaches or parents are going to blame the officials for their failures, that's very unhealthy. To me it's the equivalent of telling children they are victims, and we had way too many victims then and probably a hundred times more today.

Baseball can be a great teacher of life lessons. However, in order to play the game well, we must know the rules. There is a life rule book and it is called the Holy Bible. It is a tremendous guidebook.

The crowd in this story believed wrongly the base was a sanctuary. They thought as long as you were on the base you were safe. I fear this is the same way many folks view the church building. Many believe spending time at the church proves one is saved. Sadly, that can be far from the truth. I have heard it said that sitting in church makes you a Christian about as much as sitting in your garage makes you a car.

Matthew 7:21–23 speaks clearly to churchgoers who believe church attendance will get them to heaven. It says, "Not everyone that says to me Lord, Lord, shall enter into the kingdom of heaven; but he that does the will of my Father which is in heaven. Many will say to me in that day, Lord, Lord, have we not prophesied in your name, cast out demons and done many wonderful things? And then will I profess to them, I never knew you, depart from me you workers of iniquity."

There is only one way to heaven and that is through trusting in Jesus Christ and accepting Him as your Savior. We are all sinners and will die. However, Jesus paid for our sins by dying on a cruel cross. He definitely knows where you stand. Do you?

There is a major problem when people don't respect authority, because God is THE authority. The last thing you want to hear is the Lord say, "He's or She's Out!"

CAN I HAVE YOUR AUTOGRAPH?

CONSERVATION ENFORCEMENT OFFICERS Stewart Abrams and Jerry Fincher were on routine patrol in the far reaches of rural Coosa County when they encountered two individuals on all-terrain vehicles (ATVs) on the Paint Creek public launch area. Public launch areas were developed throughout the state to provide boaters access to waterways. These launches were normally pretty well utilized by the public and each one had a fairly long list of regulations that applied. This included no alcohol consumption, no firearm possession, no camping, and many other prohibited activities, including no ATVs. Therefore, these guys were in violation.

After a brief interview with the subjects, during which the officers pointed out the numerous signs posted around the launch area stating the rules concerning the area, the decision was made to issue citations for the illegal use of the ATVs. As the officers began writing the tickets, the younger violator noticed Jerry's name tag and asked if he was Jerry Fincher. Jerry replied he was. The young man excitedly responded, "You're the most famous game warden I know; can I have your autograph?" Jerry replied, "You are about to receive it and you can sign yours right above it!"

When Jerry shared the story with me, I had to admit it was a little disheartening seeing how I had arrested both of the individuals in the past! So much for my fame and notoriety.

You can't make this up!

NIGHT HUNTING AT THE CHICKEN HOUSES
(A LITTLE MISUNDERSTANDING)

I HAVE WRITTEN SEVERAL STORIES dealing with receiving information from the public. For an officer tasked with enforcing the game and fish laws for an entire county that might encompass four hundred to five hundred thousand acres or more, there is no substitute for receiving good information. It can make all the difference. While many cases are made as a result of an officer's use of shoe leather and perseverance, many more are made based on some good information received from the public.

While receiving any info is normally somewhat helpful, the more detailed it is the better. However, just like with many comments heard or overheard by the game warden, you must always consider the source. Sources are as varied as they can be. It may be a landowner who observed someone shining his pasture or a friend of a friend who heard about an illegally killed deer posted on Facebook. Obviously, firsthand knowledge is normally best and you might be surprised to know how often we receive a tip from someone who actually took part in a violation. Of course, friends and relatives are usually good sources; however, you must always consider their motivation.

An officer who will remain nameless received a call in the middle of the deer season from a couple who informed him their nephew was night hunting every night. This was very interesting information in that the officer had earlier received a call stating the aunt and uncle were night hunting. You might be surprised to know how often that happens. The officer asked the aunt and uncle where the night hunting was taking place and they replied it was around the chicken houses by the trailer park.

I understand everyone may not be familiar with chicken houses. Chickens and chicken products are big business in Alabama. According to the Alabama Poultry and Egg Association the poultry industry in Alabama has more than a $15 billion impact on the state and represents one-eighth of the state's economy. The industry includes everything from egg production to the production of what is normally referred to as broiler birds, which are grown for meat production.

According to the Alabama Extension System, Alabama produces twenty-three million broiler chickens each week! As you can imagine, producing twenty-three million chickens each week requires a significant number of chicken houses. Chicken houses have changed dramatically over time and fortunately have become much more efficient. In addition, they have grown in size. In general, in my area, a chicken house is normally about twelve feet high, thirty feet wide, and as much as three hundred feet long. That's a pretty big coop! There has been much research involved in developing the extremely efficient houses that are in use today. Many producers will have several houses side by side on their property. By staggering the stocking of the houses, they can know when the chickens will be ready to go to market and can manage their schedule to have the needed personnel to handle and transport the birds. While I don't know much about it, it is an interesting vocation.

Unfortunately, there is another illegal poultry enterprise that still goes on in many areas. While I have never had a chicken fight reported to me, I feel certain it still goes on. The reason I say this is that I still regularly see folks who have numerous game chicken "houses" on their property. These facilities are much different than the large commercial broiler houses where thousands of chickens reside. I guess, due to their aggressive behavior, the game chickens must have individual "houses." I have seen many styles of these houses used. Several folks use what looks like a small A-frame about three feet high while others use a thirty-gallon barrel with the end cut out. Interestingly I don't know that I have ever seen a single house on a property. The yards where I have seen these shelters normally contain as many as fifty of the small domiciles. It is an attention-grabbing sight. I find it interesting that so many people keep these chickens. Of course, my suspicious nature makes me think there is something nefarious going on; however, it is not illegal to possess the chickens.

With the information stating the night hunting was occurring near the chicken houses at the trailer park, the officer set up and worked the area a couple of nights with no success. While relaying the experience to a fellow officer he commented on how difficult it was to work night hunting in such close proximity to residences. The other officer, knowing how it sometimes smelled around a chicken house and being surprised there would be several houses nearby, asked how many chicken houses were there. The initial officer replied there were probably thirty or forty of them. This was really shocking seeing how a very large chicken operation in our area might have six to eight houses. As the second officer was scratching his head trying to figure out where there were thirty or forty chicken houses in the county, the first officer said there might not be that many but every one of the chickens had its own house. Now things were starting to come into focus.

Learning the chicken houses were game chicken houses explained a lot. These "chicken houses" were actually located in someone's yard. Now don't think for minute that a night hunter won't shoot a deer in someone's yard. However, a little deduction revealed there were two commercial chicken houses about a mile down the road from the trailer park. After learning this, the officer decided he would give the area around those chicken houses a try!

You can't make this stuff up.

BLOW IN THAT TUBE

I WASN'T SURE what I had just witnessed. It was either an amorous embrace or a molestation in progress. Either way it should not have been happening alongside US Highway 231. I knew I had to go back and check it out.

As I traveled north on the US highway that bisects rural Coosa County, I went down Hatchet Creek hill toward the narrow two-lane bridge over Hatchet Creek. On the east side of the bridge was a pull-off area where the many canoers who used the creek would often park their vehicles. I noticed a vehicle parked there and while that in itself wasn't unusual, as I passed by I looked into the vehicle and was immediately confused about what I had just witnessed. As I played it back in my mind's eye, I convinced myself there was a man and a woman in the front seat in what appeared to be an "intimate" situation. My first thought was that was an odd place to stop for a sexual interlude. While pondering that, I began to consider the situation might not be consensual. I knew our county was extremely rural; however, even if the encounter was consensual, the side of the highway wasn't the proper place for it. While this didn't necessarily fall under game and fish work, I knew it was unlikely our one deputy on duty was anywhere close. I made a U-turn in the highway and headed back toward the vehicle. As I approached the bridge, the vehicle pulled out into the road and took off at a high rate of speed.

Initiating another U-turn, I was quickly behind the vehicle and it didn't take long for me to conclude the driver was either impaired or possibly preoccupied. The driver crossed the centerline several times and appeared to be totally unable to maintain their lane. We were entering the Rockford town limit so I radioed the Rockford Police and told the officer, one of two on the force at the time, what I had. Although Rockford was the county seat of Coosa County, we were not large enough to warrant a traffic light. As a matter of fact, there was only one traffic light in the entire county! As we neared the four-way stop I could see the Rockford patrol car (the only one) coming toward us. As I was about to activate my blue lights, the driver abruptly turned into the Majik Mart, the one convenience store/gas station in the town.

The driver stopped the vehicle in front of the store and I pulled in directly behind him. Before he could exit the vehicle, I moved up to the driver's door, identified myself, and asked to see his driver's license. Although he looked to be a kid, his license showed he was nineteen years old. I noted his passenger, a young girl, appeared to be pregnant. I had the driver step out and to the rear of his vehicle. This short walk was always a pretty good indicator as to just how intoxicated someone was. I noticed he was a little unsteady but wasn't falling down. I asked what was going on back up the road and with a sheepish look he explained he and his girlfriend were on their way to the beach, which was four hours south, and had gotten a little excited and pulled over for a little intimacy. "On the side of the highway?" I asked. "Yes," was his weak answer.

While talking with the young man, I was joined by Rockford Police Officer Alan Rambo. We both detected the odor of alcoholic beverage and Alan decided to conduct a couple of field sobriety tests. Alan removed two quarters from his pocket and dropped them on the ground. He told the suspect to "pick up one of those coins." The man reached down and picked up both coins and handed them back to the officer. Alan said, "You failed the hell out of that." The boy looked at Alan with a dumbfounded look on his face. Alan administered a horizontal gaze and nystagmus test. We observed his eyes were actively twitching. Based on the results of the test, I placed the young man under arrest for driving under the influence (DUI). I explained to the girlfriend he was under arrest and told her she could follow us to the jail and I would be able to give her more information after he completed the Intoxilyzer test. I transported the teenager the one block to the county jail.

Alan prepared to administer the Intoxilyzer test while I talked with the jailer and filled out an arrest report and other booking paperwork. Alan informed me the test was ready. Although the defendant had not had a lot to say he was becoming more agitated with the situation. As I walked into the small testing room the defendant stood with the Intoxilyzer tube in his hand and Alan was finishing the implied consent paragraph he had to read before giving the test. The young man looked at me and in a belligerent tone snapped, "You can't do this, you're just a game warden." I replied, "Blow in that tube." He blew in the tube and the machine soon began printing out the results. The subject's blood alcohol level was .09. This was disheartening since .10 was the legal limit at the time. I knew it was the judge's normal practice to find any defendant whose blood alcohol content was below the limit not guilty when the case reached the court. I had figured this would probably be especially true for a young kid who had drunk just a little too much. However, he was still under arrest and would stay in jail for at least a few hours.

I returned to the booking area and told the jailer the arrestee was below the limit. I went ahead preparing the file and asked the jailer to run a criminal history on the suspect. The history came back and was not at all what I had expected. The printout revealed this was the driver's third DUI in the last six months. Obviously, there was a problem there.

During this time a third DUI conviction carried a $5,000 fine and 360 days in jail. While I was thinking the driver was very lucky to have skimmed by just below the legal limit, I was also thinking this kid obviously had a drinking problem.

The next month the case came to court. The judge called the case and the defendant and I stepped to the bench. The judge looked at the file and told the defendant he was charged with DUI and asked how he pled. I had to pick my bottom jaw up off the floor when the young man said, "Guilty, your honor." The judge also appeared to be taken back by the plea but regained his composure. He announced he would accept the guilty plea and promptly sentenced the young man to a $5,000 fine plus court costs and 360 days in jail, sixty of which had to be served.

With every DUI arrest I felt I might have saved someone's life. Normally I was thinking of the innocent driver who might be hit by the drunk. In this case, I was hopeful the time in jail might keep this kid from a life of alcoholism.

ARRESTED FOR CARRYING AN INK PEN

NO MATTER WHAT BRANCH of law enforcement you may come in contact with, it is normally true that your attitude goes a long way in having things come to a successful conclusion. Does that mean if you are respectful and forthcoming during an encounter you will walk away happy and without paperwork? No. However, if you are disrespectful and cantankerous you may be walked away in handcuffs or you may receive a handful of charges. Attitude matters.

The tone of the encounter is often set quickly. When a driver sticks their head out of their window and yells, "What the %#!* are you stopping me for?" that normally doesn't get things off on a good foot. I know it didn't this night.

A good tip is a valuable thing in the business of law enforcement. Wildlife law enforcement is no different. I have been fortunate to receive numerous good tips. I have also received some poor information. Trust me, the good ones are appreciated.

One cold December night I had responded to a complaint indicating someone was night hunting for deer in the north end of the county. The information did not include much detail but it was better than anything else I had at the time. I was soon in the area of the complaint and set up along Highway 231 in the

Hanover community in the center of Coosa County. I had contacted Conservation Enforcement Officer (CEO) Shannon Calfee and he was set up along the same road about a mile south of my location. Shannon had been working a couple of years and was therefore still very much a rookie. We kept a watch on the road and although this was a US highway traversing the county, there was little traffic. Let me tell you that situation changed unbelievably a few years later when a casino was built in the county south of ours. Having been working for thirty years prior to the casino being built, I had worked the highway many times. Normally, after about 10 p.m., you might see three or four vehicles per hour. After the Poarch Creek Indians opened the Wind Creek Casino, the traffic increased fivefold. All night long. I did not know so many people went to the casino all through the night. It definitely changed things in our county. I digress.

Shortly after I had set up surveillance in the area, I received a follow-up call which stated the vehicle I was looking for was a blue Toyota pickup. I radioed the info to Shannon. We remained in the area a while longer, however, around 11 p.m. after no contact with the vehicle we decided to head home. The forty-hour work week we were supposed to adhere to often made it difficult for us to work an area as long as we would have liked to.

Now there is evidently a rule that holds true all across the country. When a game warden decides to leave his hiding spot and pulls out on the road, no matter how many hours you have sat with not a single vehicle passing by, a vehicle will come down the road. The rule was in effect this night. I radioed Shannon and told him I was ready to go. I pulled out on the highway and Shannon was soon behind me. As fate would have it, within one mile, the first vehicle we met was—of course—a blue Toyota pickup. Once the vehicle was out of sight, I executed a U-turn and was soon approaching the slow-moving truck.

After tailing the vehicle for a short distance, the driver slowed down to about twenty miles per hour. We were northbound on the south end of Beasley Straight, a three-quarter-mile-long straight, flat stretch of highway. Obviously, the driver wanted me to pass him; however, I was where I wanted to be. A few hundred yards up the road, the driver pulled off the side of the highway. It was obvious to me someone pulling off the side of the highway near midnight was probably experiencing some type of vehicle trouble. This was before the excuse of "I just pulled off to text on my phone" became prevalent. Being the Good Samaritan I was, I pulled over behind the vehicle and, for safety purposes, activated my blue lights. Shannon pulled in behind me and we both exited our vehicles and approached the Toyota.

There were two occupants in the small truck. The driver stuck his head out the window and asked, "What's your #@!& problem?" This gracious greeting got my attention. I told the driver to place his hands on the steering wheel as I eased up to his door. I identified myself as a conservation enforcement officer and explained I thought he might have a problem seeing how slowly he was driving and the fact he had pulled off the road. He stated they were just out riding around. I asked for his driver's license, which he gave me without any further comment. The address on the license was in Montgomery, which was sixty miles south of our current location. I thought there was a little more to it than "just riding around." I asked the driver if he had any weapons and he responded he did. I asked what he had and he replied he had a pistol. "Where is it?" I asked. He responded it was "right here," pointing to a shoulder holster. I advised him to keep his hands on the steering wheel and I would retrieve the firearm. Up until now I had remained somewhat behind the subject. I now stepped up where I could get a better look in the truck. I shined my light on the passenger, a female holding a duffel bag. Protruding from the bag was the handle of a handheld spotlight. I asked if there were any other weapons in the vehicle and the driver replied "No." I told the driver I was going to remove the firearm from his holster. I took the "cocked-and-locked" .45-caliber handgun from the subject and secured it in my vehicle.

Since I had first encountered the subject, I had received a bad vibe. Having learned to trust these types of gut feelings, I was on high alert. I opened the driver's door and asked the man to exit the truck. I told him to step to the rear of the vehicle and to place his hands on the tailgate. Although verbally protesting, he reluctantly complied. I informed him I was going to handcuff him for all of our safety and did so. Folks don't like to be handcuffed; however, I have learned it is better to go ahead and handcuff them while they are at least somewhat compliant rather than when they become combative. Thankfully, I did not have to handcuff a lot of folks concerning game and fish violations. Working with the sheriff's office was a different situation!

The driver was dressed all in camo with a flashlight attached to the strap of his overalls. I felt very sure this pair were night hunting; however, I knew it would be difficult to prove it. While Shannon watched the subjects, I had the sheriff's office dispatcher run both of the people through the National Crime Information Center system at the jail. The dispatcher informed me the driver was currently under a restraining order and was not to possess any firearms. Interestingly the subject's ex-wife, the same woman who was with him in the truck, had taken out the restraining order!

I told Shannon to remove the duffel bag from the female and to search it for a weapon. No surprise to me, he found another handgun. We also found a large amount of steel wool in the truck, which piqued my interest.

I returned to the driver and asked if he was aware he was under a restraining order and not to possess any firearms. He stated the order had been dropped. I told him our records indicated it was still in effect. This immediately aggravated the subject. I was thankful I had already handcuffed the man. As his temper-fueled tirade escalated, I noticed something interesting in the pencil pocket of his overalls. There in plain view was what appeared to be the barrel of an ink pen that was somewhat melted on the end. Closer examination revealed the presence of some steel wool or Chore Boy in the melted end. I realized it was obviously being used as a drug pipe.

I have seen a little bit of everything utilized as a pipe to smoke drugs. While glass tubes or "stems" are very common, other makeshift pipes include air valves, spent rifle cartridges with the primer removed, and flattened aluminum cans. Depending on the drug being used all that was needed was a place to hold the drug so a lighter could be held to it and the air could be sucked off of it. In this case, the Chore Boy steel wool was placed in the end of the pen barrel and a crack rock would be placed on top of it. Therefore, the steel wool acted as a filter so to speak and held the rock off of the pen enough that it didn't get completely melted down. This was probably a pipe created on the spur of the moment and not intended for long-term usage.

Pointing to the drug pipe, I asked the subject, "What's this?" to which he replied, "I don't know; it's not mine!" I literally laughed out loud and asked him how he thought it had found its way into his pocket and he replied he didn't know. I informed him he was under arrest for possession of drug paraphernalia. As fate would have it, a county deputy rolled up on the scene. I asked if he would transport the subject to the jail and he did.

We questioned the female at length concerning the restraining order. She stated the order was in effect. I asked if she had come along with him voluntarily and she replied she had. We asked if they were in fact night hunting deer and she replied they were not. We released her and went to the jail and began the paperwork on the subject. The man was charged with possession of drug paraphernalia and possession of a firearm by a person forbidden to do so.

The next day I received a call from a CEO sergeant in a nearby county who inquired about the arrest the night before. He explained the female in the truck was a family friend whom he had known for many years. He shared she had called him concerning the incident and had told him I had arrested the man for possession of an ink pen. He stated he realized there was more to the case and asked if I could fill him in. I told him I had in fact arrested the man for the possession of an ink pen. I allowed that to hang in the air for a few seconds wishing I could see the look on his face. I broke the silence and asked if she had happened to mention the pen had been being used to smoke crack! He said she had somehow left that detail out. I related the remainder of details and he agreed my version made much more sense than hers.

The court date arrived and the subject and his ex-wife were each at court. His demeanor was no better than it had been on the road. The judge found the man guilty and sentenced him to fines and court costs, which he promptly paid. He quickly returned from the clerk's office and stated he wanted his guns returned immediately. His mood got noticeably worse when I informed him I would not be returning the guns to him since he was still under a restraining order forbidding him to possess firearms. It was all he could do to refrain from going totally ballistic. I explained I had checked with the Montgomery County district judge who had signed the order and she had told me the order was in effect and he was not to have the pistols. At that point, the ex-wife asked if I could turn the guns over to her. She stated the guns actually belonged to her father. I told her I would return the firearms to her, but not with the defendant present. We set up a time for her to meet me at the jail and retrieve the guns.

I typed a carefully worded release and had her sign it and gave her the firearms. While we were not able to arrest the pair for the night hunting I felt certain they were doing, we may have saved a deer or two.

The woman had called the sergeant hoping to receive some help in her ex-husband's situation. This was not at all uncommon, although no officer appreciated it. I'm sure the way the story was related to the officer he probably did have some questions. Therefore, he called me to clarify the situation not interfere with it.

Everybody gets in situations where they could use some help. Some are trivial and some are life and death. One situation is about death and eternal life. This is the one that makes all the difference. There is only one person to reach out to for help with this one. His name is Jesus. As a matter of fact, He's a good resource for whatever you are facing.

FISHING FORENSICS

WHILE EVERYBODY PROBABLY KNOWS game wardens check fishing licenses, they may not realize there are many regulations pertaining to fishing beyond just having a license. And while most probably think of someone fishing on a lake or river, there is a tremendous amount of fishing that goes on in what is considered a farm pond. I have seen "farm ponds" that range in size from a glorified mudhole to a hundred-acre lake. In Alabama, a fishing license is not required to fish in a private lake or pond. Therefore, one would probably assume we did not spend any time working at these ponds. That would be an incorrect assumption.

While you do not need a license, if the pond doesn't belong to you, you need a written permit to fish in the pond. Of course, much like hunting without a permit, if the landowner didn't care, we didn't care. However, there were plenty of landowners, especially those whose ponds could be seen from the road, who very much wanted us to check anyone fishing in their pond.

Retired game warden Byron Smith related to me an incident that occurred when he was the conservation enforcement officer (CEO) in Macon County. The owner of a large hunting lodge had contacted him complaining of two men illegally fishing in his pond. Byron soon arrived on the scene and the man told him he had eased down toward the pond to make sure they were still there and unfortunately the two had spotted him and took off running. He watched them cross the fence onto an adjacent property. Byron asked if he could recognize the men and he said he could identify the clothes they were wearing. With the landowner in tow, Byron went to where the men had crossed the fence. There on the barbed wire he found a segment of monofilament line with a sinker, hook, and worm attached. In addition, he found a wide-toothed comb lying on the ground. He collected the evidence and crossed the fence. The landowner had informed him there was a pond on the adjacent property (that he had a permit to fish in) and they were probably there. Sure enough, when they got to where they could see the pond the two men were standing on the bank each with a rod and reel in hand.

The officer and the landowner moved down the hill toward the pair. When they got close Byron turned to the landowner and asked if these were the two men. He replied they were wearing the same clothes he had observed at his lake. As they closed in on the men one of the fishermen stated, "You can't prove I was up there."

Let's pause here for a minute. As I am reviewing this story, I have been training a new officer in our county. In addition, I am preparing a training for several new officers in the department. One of the most important topics in that training is learning to listen. If an officer will really listen, a lot of folks will tell you a lot without ever realizing it. I'm sure our new officer gets tired of me going back through the conversations we have with people we check and asking him to decipher what they said. On many occasions, I have been able to see the light come on when he realizes how they actually gave themselves up without even knowing it. It's extremely important and I will continue to harp on listening!

Although it may not have been conclusive, Byron still felt the statement was basically a spontaneous exclamation of guilt.

However, since he had not seen the men fishing on the other property he knew he had better gather some more evidence. He moved to the talkative fisherman and asked him to reel his line in. The man complied and Byron examined the line, sinker, and worm and concluded they were very similar to the evidence he had collected earlier. He told the man he would be taking the line as evidence. He asked the man if he would give him a hair sample. "For what?" was the belligerent reply. "To match to the comb I found up there on the other property" was Byron's answer. Surprisingly the man reached up to his temple and pulled out some hair and handed it to the officer. Byron gathered the contact information from the men and told them he would be in touch.

Prior to becoming a CEO, Byron had worked for twelve years as a crime scene investigator and police officer in Homewood, Alabama. His training served me well. Having been through several forensics courses at Auburn University, Byron took his physical evidence to the school to have it analyzed. It ended up the evidence was sent to the wildlife forensics lab in Ashland, Oregon. The US Fish and Wildlife Service Forensics Laboratory is the only lab in the world dedicated to crimes against wildlife. The crime laboratory is very much like a "typical" police lab, except the victim is normally an animal. Their website says they "examine, identify, and compare evidence using a wide range of scientific procedures and instruments, in the attempt to link suspect, victim, and crime scene with physical evidence."

It took about six to eight weeks before he received his results. They were worth the wait. The lab said the monofilament line, the hook, and the lead sinker were all a match to what was obtained from the suspect. You may be thinking that hooks, lines, and sinkers taken from multiple people might match and you would be correct. However, of much more value, the hair in the comb matched that received from the suspect. Now that's some strong evidence. Armed with this information, Byron approached the circuit clerk and obtained warrants for fishing without a permit.

The cases were heard in district court and the judge promptly found the defendants guilty. At the conclusion of the case the judge requested that Byron meet with him in his chambers. Once in the office the judge informed Byron he could not believe anyone would go to the extent he did to make a fishing case. Byron explained he had formally been a police officer and evidence technician and continued to practice the investigation techniques he had learned there. He also explained the landowner had a lot invested in his lake and folks taking fish out of it were stealing from him and he deserved our best effort to curtail such activity. The judge commented he had never seen such effort put into a fishing case. I may be wrong but I would bet he never saw it again either.

This case makes a point that even many sportsmen miss. Anyone taking wildlife illegally is stealing it from legitimate, law-abiding sportsmen. Whether it's a thug killing a deer at night, a game hog exceeding the limit on rabbits or ducks, or a thief fishing illegally in someone's managed lake, they are each committing criminal acts. Furthermore, limits and seasons are determined in large part on the known harvest of the species. If the illegal take is significant, and it often is, it definitely can negatively affect the resource. Whether you hunt or fish or just enjoy seeing flora and fauna, wildlife outlaws are stealing from you. If you want to manage populations for future generations, report violators! Just like in this story, had the landowner not called the officer, the culprits would likely not have been apprehended. If you don't want folks stealing fish and wildlife from your property, contact your local CEO.

THIS IS YOUR LUCKY DAY

HUNTING LICENSES ARE THE LIFEBLOOD of conservation departments across the country. Many landowners and hunters mistakenly believe the Department of Conservation is funded from the state's general fund, which is funded by state tax money. I know several people believe this since several of them have claimed they pay my salary. The truth is if they aren't buying a hunting or fishing license, they likely aren't financially supporting our department. Way back in 1937 some wise men came up with the Pittman-Robinson Wildlife Restoration Act as a way to fund conservation efforts. The act placed an excise tax on firearms, ammunition, and other hunting equipment. The manufacturer pays the tax and the money goes into a fund managed by the United States Fish and Wildlife Service (USFWS). When a state Department of Conservation sells a license, the USFWS matches the cost of the license using a three-to-one match. As you can see hunters in effect pay their own way. Although hunters and fishermen pay into the fund, everyone who enjoys wildlife reaps the benefits. I feel it is safe to say that without the sale of hunting and fishing licenses conservation departments would likely cease to exist. Therefore, insuring those who are hunting and fishing are properly licensed is a high priority for game and fish departments.

While checking a fellow on the Coosa Wildlife Management Area (WMA) I asked to see his hunting license and management area license. He immediately pulled out his wallet and retrieved his hunting license. The hunting license was valid. I again asked to see his WMA license, which was also required for hunting on the area. The man was starting to get upset because he was positive he had purchased the license yet was having trouble finding it. Of course, this would not be the first time someone had sworn to me they had purchased a license when they had not. Many people do not understand why officers do not believe them when they tell them they have everything they need. If they were lied to as much as we are, I feel they would better understand. While I did not necessarily doubt whether or not he had purchased the license, it was beginning to look like he wasn't going to find it.

Eventually he took everything out of his wallet and the contents nearly covered the hood of his truck! Yet, he still could not find the necessary license. After the fellow had spent several minutes searching his wallet and his vehicle but still could not find the document, I told him I was going to issue him a citation. I explained if he could later prove he had the license prior to receiving the ticket, I would request the ticket be dismissed. He wasn't happy but stated he understood. I asked for his driver's license and he handed it to me. I took the license and as I rotated it in my hand I noticed the back of the license was not slick like the front. I flipped the license over and there stuck on the back of his driver's license was, you guessed it, his WMA license! I held the license up and asked the fellow, "Does this look like it?" He was sure happy to see it and, to tell the truth, so was I. It was definitely his lucky day!

Have you ever had a lucky day like that? Maybe you thought you were getting a speeding ticket and the trooper returned with a written warning or you saw the blue lights behind you but they pulled over the car in front of you. The truth is today may very well be your lucky day. You woke up this morning. You had time today to read this book at your leisure. The Bible says life is short and full of troubles. You've likely experienced that as well. It also says all have sinned and come short of the glory of God (Romans 3:23). It teaches there is a heaven and a hell and we will all spend eternity in one of those two places. God offers us salvation through his son, Jesus Christ. It's up to us to accept it. You can do that today. Romans 6:23 says the wages of sin is death, but the gift of God is eternal life through Jesus Christ our Lord. Romans 10:9–10 says, if you believe in your heart and confess with your mouth that Jesus is Lord and was raised from the dead, you will be saved. Do that, and this will be your lucky day!

LASER SURGERY

WHILE ON PATROL as a reserve deputy for the Coosa County Sheriff's Office I was accompanying Deputy Mike Rudd en route to serve a felony warrant with a $100,000 bond. Warrants with that amount of bond were pretty unusual and it was normally a good idea to have a little backup when attempting to serve the individual. We had contacted Deputy Josh Jones and asked him to accompany us. As we neared the residence we met a vehicle without any taillights. Josh turned around and pursued the vehicle. Knowing the most insignificant traffic stop could easily turn into a life-and-death encounter in the blink of an eye, we followed to back him up. Although we all handled many calls by ourselves it felt good when there was backup available.

The vehicle with no taillights turned into a driveway and Josh activated his blue lights. We all approached the vehicle. Deputy Jones requested the man's driver's license and he replied he did not have one. Although he knew it wasn't, Josh asked if this was the man's residence and he said it was not. He asked who lived at the residence and the man replied it was his brother's residence. Being familiar with both the driver and the homeowner, Deputy Jones informed the man that he knew this wasn't his brother's residence. The man immediately changed his story and said the person living there was actually his friend. When asked the name of his friend he first replied, "Pauko." He then quickly changed the name to Johnny. It was obvious the man had no idea who lived there but was only trying to duck away from the officer. At this point two people exited the residence. We asked if they knew the driver of the vehicle and they replied they did not.

Many times, violators will pull into a driveway in an effort to elude an officer. I have witnessed it tried several times; however, I rarely remember it working. Violators often fail to realize the officers in rural counties often know the vast majority of the residents and who lives where. Yet I learned a long time ago people will do and try anything.

Realizing his ruse had not worked, the driver began to complain he didn't know what this was all about since he had not done anything wrong. We explained it was in fact wrong to drive a car without any taillights and with no driver's license and to lie to law enforcement officers. In addition, we smelled the aroma of alcoholic beverage emanating from the man. When asked how much he had had to drink, he contemplated for a minute and replied, "A six pack." I asked the man where he was coming from and he replied, "My girlfriend's house." I asked where he was going and he replied, "Home to my wife." You can't make this stuff up.

Josh told the man he wanted him to perform some tests to determine whether or not he was too impaired to drive. The deputy explained and demonstrated the heel-to-toe walking test. The man attempted the test and although he didn't fall down, to say he passed it would be a stretch. Deputy Jones instructed the man to perform a one-legged stand by lifting one foot six inches off the ground and counting to thirty. The man quickly replied he couldn't do that. When asked why, the fellow pulled up his left pants leg and stated, "I had surgery on my leg." I illuminated his leg with my flashlight and saw the man did indeed have a bad

LASER SURGERY

scar just below the knee. The scar was obviously pretty old. When Josh asked him when he had the surgery he said, "Last week." Somewhat stunned, Josh said, "You had surgery last week and you already have a scar?" The man replied, "Yeah, it was laser surgery and them things are hot!" It was all I could do not to bust out laughing.

Sensing the man would not be able to perform any further tests the deputy asked him to blow in the portable breath tester. After several attempts the man finally provided a sufficient sample and the machine revealed his blood alcohol was .12, which was one and a half times the legal limit. The man was placed under arrest and taken to jail where he refused the Dräger breath analysis. Fortunately, I've never had to have laser surgery, but if I do I'm going to remember, those things are HOT!

THE BIGGEST TURKEY IN THE COUNTY

Working turkey bait was very often a time-consuming and frustrating proposition. About twelve to fourteen years into my career, a local "hunting celebrity" was arrested for hunting over bait. The trial resulted in a significant change in what it would take to earn a conviction in a hunting-by-the-aid-of-bait case. The phrase "knew or should have known" was added to the Alabama baiting law. This meant just because someone was sitting in a baited area, they couldn't be arrested unless you could prove to the judge they knew or should have known the bait was there. This didn't have a profound effect on deer baiting since the hunters normally sat watching the bait, but for turkey hunters it meant they could spread bait in the area and as long as they weren't sitting right over it, it would be more difficult to make a case. More difficult, but still doable.

One reason working turkey bait was aggravating was that being on bait at daylight meant I couldn't be hunting at daylight. Like many in my profession, I enjoyed hunting and the outdoors. Many times in my career I had people comment they wished they had a job where they could hunt and fish all the time, while others would say it must be nice to be able to hunt wherever I wanted to. Of course both of those assumptions were very far from the truth. Most of the time when people were hunting, I was working.

I long ago conceded I would basically forfeit hunting during most of the deer season. Early in my career, it wasn't at all unusual to work sixty to seventy hours a week during the deer season. For several years Coosa was the northernmost county in the state to have a good deer population. That meant folks from north Alabama, where deer were scarce, flooded into the county to hunt deer. That influx of folks, combined with our local hunters, kept things hopping from October through January. Believe me when I tell you we were pretty well whipped by the end of the season. We would normally try to recuperate during the month of February—that is until the deer season was extended to February 10!

Since my deer-hunting time was limited, I did my best not to miss many days of the turkey season. Unfortunately, sometimes it couldn't be avoided. This was especially true after our two veteran officers retired. Having been in the county for fifteen years, I had developed relationships with many county residents and now received the majority of the complaints in the county. During this time, I often found myself working with new officers who had little or no experience. Such was the case during the turkey season in 2003.

Although enforcement was not my primary job, I had always worked it diligently and now it was more important than ever that people received a response when they complained. For any young officers reading this, the quickest way to quit receiving any information from the public is not to act on what you receive. Although many people would overlook some illegal deer hunting, when someone's illegal activity started affecting another's turkey hunting, people started complaining.

Since turkey season coincided with Little League baseball season, I often compared notes on the morning's hunts with the other coaches at practice each afternoon. It was at one of these practices that our team manager shared with me his suspicion that some illegal activity was taking place on a property adjacent to his. I told him I would try to check it out.

Fortunately, a coworker had leased the property adjacent to the suspect's, which significantly reduced my walk into the property the next morning. I eased onto the property and began walking a logging road looking for any evidence that something sinister might be afoot. Having never been on the property before, I had to take it slow and pay close attention. Coming to a fork in the road, I went to the right and soon came into an opening containing a small lake. As I walked along the side of the lake I began to hear the sound of turkeys scratching in the leaves. I slipped over a small rise and spotted a gobbler as he scratched in the leaves about thirty yards in front of me. As I watched the gobbler, a hen's head suddenly appeared midway between us. She quickly decided I didn't belong there and she putted and made a loud and raucous exit. The woods then exploded with at least two big gobblers and several hens flying through the trees. I walked over to the area where all of the scratching was taking place and was not surprised to find cracked corn scattered in the leaves. I gathered a sample of the bait and continued to scout the property. Experience had taught me while some baiters would only bait one spot, others would bait several areas. Therefore, I kept looking.

I returned to the fork in the road and took the left fork. Before long I found another area where the leaves had been thoroughly scattered. A little searching on my part again revealed cracked corn. I took another sample and, finding no other baited areas, left the property.

I called our new conservation enforcement officer (CEO) and told him we had some bait to work. We decided to check the area the next morning. Shannon was not a turkey hunter and as a new officer had never worked any turkey bait. Unfortunately this bait would not be easy to work since the hunter evidently wasn't hunting from a blind or specific location. Since the property had multiple baited sites, we would have to try and determine where the hunter was entering the property and which area he would be in.

The next day I met Shannon and showed him the baited areas. We investigated a little further and determined there were a couple of four-wheeler trails leading into the area. We had an idea which house the hunter was staying in when he visited but did not know his name or when he was hunting. We alternated checking the area each day to no avail.

A few days later at ball practice, the team manager told me I should have been on the property that morning. I told him Shannon had been on the property. He stated someone had shot on the property at about 9:00 a.m. That night I phoned Shannon and asked if he had worked the bait and he said he had. When I told him someone had shot on the property around nine in the morning, he said he had left the property an hour before that. I told him he needed to go back in the morning and stay until at least ten. I explained baiters would often hunt a gobbling turkey on the roost and would then move to the baited area later in the morning. He told me he would be there in the morning.

The next afternoon, I met Shannon and he told me he had an unbelievable story. Fearing he had been caught checking the area, I said, "Let's hear it." Little did I know it would be one of the most outlandish stories I had ever heard. He said he entered the area at daylight and stayed in place until after nine o'clock. When no one showed, he decided to check the west side of the property and see if any bait had been added to that site. While surveying the area, he heard a rumbling that he soon realized was a four-wheeler and it was quickly closing in on him! Unfortunately he was in an open area and would not be able to make it to cover before the four-wheeler rider would be able to see him. With nowhere to go, he dove into the dead leaves beside the four-wheeler trail and hoped the guy would take another route.

Getting "caught" working bait was the worst. Every time we checked a property we ran the risk of being spotted. And being spotted by someone who wasn't hunting at the time usually led to the bait and the hunting drying up. Take it from me, when you have made numerous trips, which sometimes could be a mile-long walk, into a property, you definitely wanted to end that scenario with the apprehension of the suspect. When it ended with your being apprehended, it was aggravating to say the least. I felt certain I was about to hear such a sad tale.

Shannon stated as he laid in the leaves the rider steadily approached. It appeared evident he had been spotted since the guy was headed straight for him. Frustrated, he contemplated standing up and confronting the guy. While quickly debating his next move, his frustration turned to concern, as it appeared the vehicle was headed directly at him. Lying on his back on the ground in full uniform with no camouflage he could not believe it when the man passed by him at less than ten feet and evidently never saw him! Although he seemed to have avoided detection, unfortunately the trail ended about twenty yards ahead and he knew the fellow would have to ride right back past him and it was only a matter of time until he would be discovered. However, he decided to remain motionless and see what transpired.

The rider stopped the four-wheeler approximately ten yards past Shannon's location and dismounted. The officer observed as the fellow walked in front of the ATV and filled a gallon can with cracked corn from a sack on the front rack. The man then began to scatter the cracked corn throughout the area. Shannon said he could not believe it when the man actually slung corn on him. Literally, he threw corn onto the officer who lay on his back in the leaves alongside the trail. The fellow then remounted the ATV and once again drove right past the motionless game warden. When he finished the story, I simply said, "You are right." He looked at me with a puzzled look on his face and I told him he was right when he said he had a story I wouldn't believe because I didn't believe it! He assured me it was the truth and I told him he had better write it down because he would probably never have anything like that happen again.

We decided we would work the area jointly the next morning and attempt to apprehend the violator. Our plan was for me to wait near the baited area and Shannon would wait at the entrance to the property. Once the violator entered, Shannon could radio me and let me know which area the hunter was headed toward and I could hopefully be waiting there when he arrived.

The next morning I was in position well before daylight. As I stood in the cool morning air I soon heard the hum of a four-wheeler as it approached my location. I radioed Shannon and asked which way the guy was headed but received no answer. Soon the noise stopped. I began watching for someone on foot. This type of ambush was dangerous. I was wearing a camo jacket and was waiting on an armed violator who I was sure would be in full camo in the woods with very low light. I positioned myself beside a large tree and waited. Repeated tries to reach Shannon were unsuccessful. Soon I heard muffled voices. I knew this meant one of two things. Either the officer had already apprehended the guy and was bringing him toward me or there were multiple hunters. In the dim light of the dawn, I soon made out the silhouettes of two hunters as they approached my location. As they closed the distance between us, I decided to employ a technique I had used several times in the past. I had learned early on it wasn't wise to startle anyone walking through the woods with a loaded firearm. Once the pair passed my location, I whistled. At the sound of the whistle the duo stopped dead still and listened. I took that opportunity to identify myself as the state game warden and told them to place their guns on the ground. They complied.

I approached them and asked if they possessed any other weapons. They stated they did not and I quickly patted them down and then moved over and retrieved and unloaded their guns. I again attempted to reach Shannon on the radio but received no reply. I had no choice but to proceed without him. I asked both men for their licenses and permits. As he was retrieving his license, the older of the two explained we were on his family's property and the fellow with him was his guest. About that time a turkey began gobbling about 150 yards from our position. I looked at the licenses and again called Shannon on the radio but got no answer. I read the men their rights and told them I wanted to ask them some questions. I moved the property owner up the trail with me so the guest could not hear our conversation. I asked the man if he hunted the property regularly and he stated this was his first trip to the property since he had suffered a heart attack the previous year. He explained he had gotten the go-ahead from his doctor if he would use a 20-gauge shotgun. If this was true, it meant our bait case was going out the window since he couldn't have baited the property if this was his first visit. However, this also wouldn't be the first time I'd been lied to!

I asked who else had permission to hunt the property and he confirmed no one else should be hunting it. I began to suspect he was not necessarily being straight with me. As the gobbler continued to gobble, I again called Shannon and finally got a response. He advised he was headed my way. The fellow asked me what the problem was and I advised him I had another officer on the property and needed to speak with him. I heard Shannon approaching and began walking toward him with the fellow following behind me. I made eye contact with Shannon and in front of my body I pointed toward the man and then gave him the look that asked the question "Is this the right guy?" Fortunately, the young officer understood what I wanted to know and nodded his head yes. I breathed a huge sigh of relief.

I turned to the fellow and told him the reason we were here was the area was baited and I asked if he knew anything about it. He hesitated and then said he did not know about it. His hesitation told me a lot. I gave him my best "I know you're lying" stare. While this technique didn't always work, silence was often more than a violator could take. After a few seconds, I asked the man what he would say if I told him I had someone who had seen him putting the bait out on the property. He immediately confessed. I placed him under arrest.

I pulled Shannon to the side and told him we wouldn't have anything on the other fellow if he didn't admit knowing the bait was there. I told him to go ahead and start writing the first subject while I talked with the guest. I went to the second guy and simply asked him if he knew the property was baited and he replied, "Yeah, I know it." I then advised him he was under arrest. While we wrote the citations, the gobbler continued to tear the woods up with multiple gobbles. We finished with the tickets and explained the area could not be hunted until after the bait had been gone for ten days. The fellow apologized for baiting the area and thanked us.

As Shannon and I walked back to the truck, I told him I really wasn't worried that the guy would have killed any turkeys. When he asked why, I told him to think about it. The guy had thrown corn on the biggest turkey in the county and didn't get him! He really appreciated that.

I may be wrong, but I think you would have to look long and hard to find a more incredible first turkey-baiting case!

PETA CALLING

AS A LIFELONG HUNTER, a wildlife biologist, and a Christian who believes God gave man dominion over all creation, I enjoy hunting and eating wild game and have a hard time understanding anyone who doesn't. Although I'm sure there are well-meaning people who are members of animal rights groups, I'm convinced the leadership of many of these groups are wackos! I watched on television as a leader of one such group held a chicken and looked into the camera and said, "When I look in this chicken's eyes, I see a child's eyes." Wow! I was very fortunate in that I had basically no contact with these groups during my career. However, I did have an interesting indirect contact.

In the fall of 2005 the Coosa County Sheriff's Office (SO) received a call from a representative of People for the Ethical Treatment of Animals (PETA) in New York City. The caller stated they had (somehow) been made aware of an egregious practice taking place at a hunting preserve in the eastern part of the county. A little information is needed for you to grasp this situation. The Coosa County SO is located in Rockford, the county seat, which currently has a population of maybe four hundred people. The entire county has a population of just over ten thousand. There is one traffic light in the county. We don't encounter too many New Yorkers! Therefore, you can see how a communication barrier might possibly exist between the caller from New York City and the one taking the call. As a matter of fact, I'm sure when they heard *New York City* they probably didn't hear the rest of it the first time through. We didn't get many calls from there and didn't want to.

However, the caller stated they had been informed the members and guests at the shooting club known as Five Star were taking part in a sadistic pigeon hunt and as if that wasn't bad enough the members were breaking the bird's wings prior to shooting them. I must admit upon hearing this report my first impulse was to laugh out loud. Not because someone breaking a bird's wings was at all humorous but because picturing anyone breaking a bird's wings and then either pitching them in the air or shooting them as they walked on the ground was beyond ludicrous.

Of course this type of dastardly conduct must be investigated and our county game warden was notified and responded immediately. We were both very familiar with the facility. It was a high-dollar hunting operation that would release over one hundred thousand birds for hunting each year. However, we had no idea they might be breaking the wings prior to releasing the birds!

The officer investigated the call and shockingly found it to be unfounded. Although they were having a shoot, the birds' wings were not broken and the pheasants were really flying good. As the property manager escorted him from one hunter to the next he was a little surprised when the manager asked, "Have you ever met Colonel Oliver North?" The officer replied he had not; however, that changed when he made his acquaintance at the next stand. After I learned who was in attendance I better understood why we received the call in the first place! It sounds like there may have been more than one kind of "pigeon" at that shoot.

GUILTY AS CHARGED

IT'S A GOOD THING this guy wasn't Pinocchio because if he was, his nose would have likely poked my eye out. Although he struggled for a good excuse, the guilt hung on him like a cheap suit.

The vast majority of cases made by conservation enforcement officers (CEO) were on-view arrests, meaning the violation occurred in the presence of the officer. While it is easy to understand how most of our cases happened that way, I always enjoyed taking a little evidence and information and making a good case out of it. For whatever reason it was the view of many of the officers in the field that the powers that be in our Montgomery office didn't want the officers *wasting their time* on investigations when there were plenty of on-view cases that could be and needed to be made.

One thing I picked up on early in my career was the officers I worked with took the cases they made personally. One reason was the time and effort it took to make many of our cases. Depending on the type of case, we have spent weeks, months, and even years trying to apprehend someone. Losing any case was hard to swallow; however, losing one in which we had a lot of time and effort invested really left a bitter taste. I quickly realized the only power I had to ensure I would not lose a case was to make the best possible case. While even the best case could be lost, for the most part, a well-made case would stand up in court. I vowed early on that if I was to lose a case it would not be because I failed to do my best. That thinking served me well for over thirty years. Another reason we took our cases personally was, as Terry Grosz put it, we were a sword for Mother Nature representing wildlife that died without making a sound. The CEO is the front line of defense for America's wildlife resources.

Around noon on the first Saturday of the 2005 Alabama spring wild turkey season, I received a call from the Coosa County Sheriff's Office (SO) dispatcher stating someone had shot a turkey from the road on Alabama Highway 22 just west of Rockford. Although I was off duty, I told the dispatcher I would attempt to contact one of the two county game wardens. My new position as a private lands biologist for central Alabama was in full swing. Traversing the twenty-three counties I was assigned was taking its toll and although I was putting in over fifty hours a week on average, it was still difficult to cover everything. This position had basically eliminated any time for law enforcement, a situation I wasn't very happy about. I turned on my radio and contacted our two officers and found they were both in an adjacent county. Since I always consider violations against turkeys especially heinous, I decided I would answer the call.

I drove to the jail and spoke directly with the dispatcher and gathered all the possible details. He informed me a neighbor had witnessed the incident and had been able to get a tag number off the suspect vehicle. Wow, what a great bit of info—or so I thought. I asked who the vehicle was registered to and he replied it had come back not on file. Tags that came back not on file were frustrating. There were several reasons why this would happen with one of the most common reasons being the tag had been read incorrectly. I hoped this hadn't occurred and told the dispatcher I would double-check with the witness.

HE'S STILL SHOOTING

I left the jail and headed to the area where the shooting from the public road violation had occurred. Coosa County Alabama is 92 percent forested. The only open areas in the county are pastures, some with cattle and some without. The property where the alleged incident had taken place was one of the few cattle pastures that bordered the Alabama highway that bisected the county.

I arrived at the complainant's property and attempted to locate the landowner with no success. I went down the highway to visit the neighbor who had witnessed the incident. I spotted him in his yard and pulled into the driveway. I was familiar with the guy seeing how we had coached Little League together for the past couple of years. After a brief greeting, I told him I was here to investigate the incident that had occurred earlier in the day and asked what he could tell me about it. He stated he had been in his dad's yard when he heard a vehicle pull into the gravel parking lot of the church just east of his location. He looked toward the church and observed a black Nissan Titan pickup as it turned around in the parking lot. The Titan was a new model that had just been out for a year or so and had a distinctive look. He said the vehicle had simply turned around and headed back east toward Rockford. Within about a minute, he heard a gunshot. He said he told his dad he thought the shot was on the neighboring property and they both jumped in his truck to go and investigate. As he backed toward the road, he again saw the black Nissan Titan as it came from the east. He stated the vehicle passed directly by him and it was occupied by one white male. I asked if he got the tag number and he said he did and it was very distinctive. The plate read GOBLIN.

He stated he drove toward where he had heard the shot. When he reached the church, he met the neighboring landowner, who was driving toward him. He pulled to the side of the road and his neighbor told him the guy in the black truck had just shot a turkey in his field. With that info, he decided to try to catch the vehicle. After a brief one-hundred-miler-per-hour run down the highway without spotting the truck, he decided to terminate the pursuit. I asked him if he had seen any other vehicles on the road between the time he first saw the Nissan and when it came by him. He replied there were no other vehicles on the road except for him and his neighbor. I thanked him for his assistance and told him I would be in touch.

    I went back to the landowner's home and this time found him there. I had met this fellow before but did not really know him. I introduced myself and told him I understood he had experienced a little excitement earlier in the day. He said he had. I asked him to give me the details of the event. He stated he and his wife were in their van in their driveway when they observed a black Nissan Titan pickup traveling toward the west at a slow rate of speed. As they watched, the vehicle pulled off the left side of the road adjacent to their pasture. They were approximately 150 yards away when they saw what they first thought was the man's arm out the driver's window. However, when they heard the shot, they realized the man had a gun out the window. After the shot they saw a turkey as it began flopping at the edge of the woods. The landowner immediately headed toward the truck. The driver/shooter took off to the west with the landowner in pursuit. He said when he reached the top of the hill he met his neighbor (the fellow I had spoken with earlier) and told him the guy had just shot a turkey and his neighbor then took up the pursuit. I asked him how many people were in the truck and he said there was only one occupant. I asked if he got the tag number and he replied he did not get close enough to read it. When asked if there were any other vehicles on the road he emphatically answered, "No!" I asked if he was sure of the make of the vehicle and he stated he had been an automotive mechanic for fifteen years and he was 100 percent certain it was a Nissan Titan pickup.

I asked what happened next and he explained he went back to the field and attempted to retrieve the turkey. However, the turkey was not dead and they ended up chasing the wounded bird through the woods for over an hour but could not catch it. I told him it would not be an easy case, but I would do the best I could with it.

I returned to the jail and got with the dispatcher and we again ran the tag and it again came back not on file. We tried numerous possible spellings but could not come up with anything that would match. I asked the dispatcher if he was familiar with having the Alabama Criminal Justice Information Center (ACJIC) run an offline search. I explained I had in the past contacted the ACJIC and gave them a partial tag and they found all possible matches for me. We rummaged around and came up with a number and called the ACJIC. Seeing how it was Saturday afternoon, I was definitely surprised when the call was answered. Interestingly it turned out the lady on the line was the same person I had talked with years before. We explained we were pretty sure we had the tag correct but it continued to come back as not on file. She said she would be able to help us but it would be Monday before she could access the computer. She explained she was off duty but had transferred her work phone to her house. She said she would fax the results to me via the jail. I must admit that was going above and beyond and I definitely appreciated it.

On Monday I contacted the jail and asked if they had received a fax from the ACJIC and was told they had not. This was disappointing in that it probably meant things weren't going to go very well. On Tuesday evening I stopped by the jail and checked to see if they had received anything. The dispatcher checked the box and sure enough I had a fax. I immediately looked at the page and found the tag GOBLIN should be displayed on a 2004 Nissan Titan, black in color. It also contained the name and address of the owner. Now we were cooking with gas. I called my local game warden, Shannon Calfee, and told him I had some good information concerning the turkey shooting case and we needed to go and interview somebody. We began trying to mesh our schedules, which with me traveling across twenty-three counties was difficult to do.

More than a week had passed before we could attempt to interview the subject. We traveled to the adjacent county and after a little searching located the man's home. I had not contacted the man previously. I wanted to "catch him cold" so he would not have his answers prepared. Listening to how people answer questions is probably one of the most important aspects of law enforcement work. I normally thoroughly enjoyed interviewing and interrogating subjects. While I wished I had received more training than I had, our department wasn't very high on it. Therefore, I had gleaned what I could from our training and had supplemented it with study on my own and by working with the Coosa County Sheriff's Office investigator. I learned although each person was different, everyone does many things the same way. Sometimes you would get shut down by a suspect, but normally you could learn a good bit.

As we pulled in the driveway, the man walked out of his house and met us in the carport area, next to a black Titan pickup. The fellow appeared to be in his fifties, heavyset, with thinning salt-and-pepper hair. I introduced Shannon and myself and told him we were from Coosa County and investigating an incident that had occurred there. I informed him we would like to ask him some questions and I advised him of his rights by reading him the Miranda warning. I hated to have to do that since I knew if a law enforcement officer pulled up in my driveway and began by reading me my rights I probably would be very suspect as to what he was up to and probably pretty tight lipped. However, I had also learned if someone did not appear at least inquisitive about why they were being advised of their rights, they probably knew why.

I began by asking the man if he was in Coosa County on March 19. He first said yes, but then said he wasn't sure. He went on to say he hunted all over the state and just couldn't remember where he was that Saturday. I inquired as to where he hunted in Coosa County and he replied he hunted on the McConnell property near Rockford. I was very familiar with the property. I asked if the black Nissan Titan with the license plate GOBLIN, which he was currently leaning on, belonged to him and he said it did. I explained we were investigating a report of someone shooting a turkey from the road in Coosa County on March 19. This did not really get any response from him verbally; however, his failure to respond spoke volumes to me. I asked if he had been hunting on the McConnell property on Saturday, March 19, and he again responded he just really couldn't remember. It was now time to get serious. I looked him square in the eye and I said, "I think you would remember if you shot a turkey out of the window!" There was a brief hesitation, which again spoke volumes, and the man said he didn't do that. He went on to say he had killed turkeys all over the state and had several mounted in his house and he didn't need to shoot one from the road. He added he had worked closely with the turkey federation and with the Becoming an Outdoors-Woman program and several groups. What he said was interesting, but not as much as what he didn't say. He did not emphatically state he did not do what I was accusing him of. Once again this told me something.

I decided to move on and I asked the man, who I now viewed as a defendant, if anyone else could have been driving his truck on the date in question. That received the emphatic statement, "No one drives that truck but me!" That statement would prove to be pivotal. I informed him I had three witnesses that would testify someone in his truck had stopped and shot a turkey from the road. He still did not deny having done it. I asked, "Why do you think someone would be willing to sign a warrant on you for shooting from the road?" He thought for a moment and responded he had to drive a lot in his job and he may have cut someone off in traffic and they may have got mad and done this. I must admit in all my years in law enforcement this was a new one. I looked at the man and asked if he really thought someone would sign a warrant against him for shooting a turkey from the road because he had cut them off in traffic. He replied that was the only reason he could think of. I thought to myself I hope this is the defense he uses in court!

I informed him the witnesses were very firm in their statements about what had happened. I let that hang in the air as I waited for his response. He thought for a moment and said he just didn't understand it because he had not done it. He went on to say he was a deacon in the Baptist church and he just didn't do things like that. I did not respond to his statement. There were a couple of reasons why. Reason one was I was about 75 percent sure he was guilty of the offenses and reason two was I was a deacon in a Baptist church and it really bothered me that someone who I felt certain was lying would use that as a defense.

As I was ruminating on what he had said and deciding what to say next, he asked a question that, for me, was the clincher. He looked at me and asked, "Did they get the turkey?" At that moment I declared the man guilty in my mind. Let me tell you why. What if I came to your house and accused you of shooting a turkey from the road? Most people who were not guilty would take offense to something like that. Would you? This guy didn't take offense; instead, he asked if they got the turkey. This also told me he knew he didn't kill the turkey cleanly.

Confident we had gained enough information to further the investigation, we wrapped up the interview and told him we would be back in touch. He said to be sure and let him know how it turned out and I told him I was sure we would let him know.

Shannon and I returned to our vehicle and once inside I looked at Shannon and said, "Guilty as sin." Shannon responded, "You are so right!" I immediately got on the phone and contacted Doug McConnell. Doug was the co-owner and caretaker of the McConnell property in Rockford. I asked whether or not the man was a member of their hunting club and he verified he was. I asked if he knew if the man had hunted there on Saturday, March 19. He stated he remembered the fellow had hunted there that day and he had hunted right behind the cabin where Doug was making some repairs. I asked if they maintained a sign-in-and-out sheet and he replied they did. He went on to say the man had signed out around 10:15 a.m.; however, he had gone to scout an area and actually did not leave the property until probably 11:30 or so. This was important information since the road-hunting incident had occurred just before noon and was about ten to fifteen minutes from the McConnell property. Things were coming together. I informed Doug we were conducting an investigation and we would be coming by for a copy of the sign-in/-out log.

I decided to reinterview the witnesses and make sure things were as they seemed. I spoke with each witness separately and got the same story again and obtained written statements. Each witness was positive the truck was a black Nissan Titan. Armed with statements from the witnesses, a statement from Doug McConnell, and a copy of the sign-in/-out log from the hunting club, I was ready to approach the clerk and sign some warrants. I met with the clerk and explained what evidence I had obtained and told him I wanted to sign warrants for hunting from the public road, hunting by aid of a vehicle, and hunting without a permit. He concurred and I soon had the warrants in hand.

I contacted Shannon and informed him I had the warrants and planned to ask the defendant to meet me at the jail on Saturday. I contacted the defendant and told him I would like to meet with him again. He stated he would also like to get this matter cleared up. I told him I would like to meet on Saturday and he stated he would be out of town. I told him I would attempt to set up another date but it might be a week or two. I assured him I would be in touch. I called Shannon and told him what had transpired and we would try again later.

About twenty minutes later, my phone rang and caller ID showed it was the defendant. The fellow told me he had changed his plans and would like to meet on Saturday. I told him that would be good and to meet me at the Coosa County jail in Rockford at noon. He hesitated and said he didn't want to meet at the jail. He asked if we could meet at the hunting club and I told him no, I would rather meet at the jail. He said coming to the jail would make him feel like a criminal. I held my tongue on what I wanted to say and told him it would be best to have a room where we could sit down and on a Saturday in Rockford the jail was the only place that was open. He reluctantly agreed.

Saturday rolled around and Shannon and I arrived at the jail thirty minutes early and found the defendant and his wife waiting on us. We entered the jail and moved through the series of heavy metal doors with electronic locks and soon arrived at a small library/interrogation room. I again advised the man of his rights and began asking a series of questions I had written out. I recorded all of his answers and asked him to sign the page and he did. At that point, I advised him based on the information gathered during the investigation I had obtained warrants for his arrest on three charges. I explained the charges and the bonding procedure. When I finished my explanation, I allowed the man to sign his bonds. The defendant asked what I thought he should do and I explained I could not offer him any legal advice. I told him he could either appear in court or contact the judge and he might allow him to handle it through the mail.

The defendant's wife stated she worked for the largest law firm in the state and legal representation would not be a problem. I told her that would be fine. She added her husband could not have done this because he was at home by the time this had occurred. In light of that statement, I found what she asked next to be quite interesting. She wanted to know if her husband could not just pay a fine on this. I told her he could and that was the way this was normally handled. The defendant asked if he would have to plead guilty to pay it off and I told him he would. He said he wasn't going to plead guilty to something he did not do. (I wish I had a dollar for every time a defendant had said that.) He added he just didn't understand why someone would sign a warrant against him for this. He stated all he could think of was he must have cut someone off in traffic and they had gotten his tag and signed a warrant. This was the third time he had told me this and I had heard it more than enough. I told him I had been doing this type of work for nineteen years and I had never had anyone sign a warrant on someone for shooting a turkey from the road because they had cut them off in traffic. I went on to inform him I did not believe that anyone ever would do that. I was again thinking if this was going to be his defense in court, this might be a lot easier than I thought. He said he just did not understand the whole ordeal. I told him we would get it all straightened out in court the next month. With that, we left the jail.

Shannon and I agreed things had gone fairly well and now we would soon face our next obstacle. This obstacle was one we should not have had to get over; however, it was an obstacle I had fought for my entire career. I'm sad to say that obstacle was our assistant district attorney (ADA).

Everyone who has watched the plethora of law-and-order type shows on television knows that the district attorney takes the case from the officers, examines and furthers the investigation, and eventually brings the defendant to justice. Well that is how it normally works on television; unfortunately, I was dealing with real life and a part-time ADA whose day job was being a defense attorney. One thing I did know was if I could get it by the ADA, winning the case would be a cinch. Maybe that's why he was the way he was. I did not appreciate him giving me such a hard time but I must admit it caused me to make better, more thorough cases. That may have been his angle.

Tuesday of the following week, I received a call from the jail stating that the ADA would like to meet with me. In my experience, lawyers were like anyone else in that they all had friends in the business and often wanted to help one another out. I feared this definitely would be the case when dealing with the largest firm in the state. However, I felt I had done my very best preparing the case and was ready to see how it went. I dropped by the ADA's office the next day. The attorney cut right to the chase and said he understood I had arrested a man for hunting from the road, by aid of a vehicle, and without a permit. He asked me to give him the gist of what had occurred. I began with the call from the SO and did my best not to leave out any details. When I told him I had a couple of witnesses, he stopped me and asked if either witness could positively identify the man in the vehicle. I knew this would be his question as I knew it was a legitimate concern. I was ready and told him they could not identify him; however, I felt I had sufficient evidence to prove he was the man in the truck. I relayed every detail, especially the man's statement that no one drove the truck but him. I wrapped up the evidence and asked the attorney what he thought. He looked at me and said, "If it goes to court, he'll be convicted." I must admit that statement made my day. Not only because the man would be convicted but that the ADA felt that way about it. He told me a lawyer with the big law firm had called him and inquired about the case. The attorney stated the defendant had claimed he did not commit the offenses but they would entertain a plea bargain. I asked what that indicated to him and he just looked at me and smiled. He asked what we could offer them to settle the case. This always irritated me because I always felt the defendants were guilty of everything I wrote them for, otherwise I wouldn't have arrested them. However, experience had taught me how to handle the situation and that was why I had brought the three charges against the man. I told him we could drop the hunting-by-aid-of-a-vehicle charge and would accept a minimum fine and costs on the other two. He told me he would contact the attorney and would let me know.

A couple of days passed and I received word the offer had been accepted. The plea contained so much legalize it literally filled two typed pages. However, the bottom line was the defendant pled guilty and paid fines and court costs totaling $938.

After this case, I received a comment that to me was a huge compliment. A fellow officer told me, "There aren't three game wardens in this state that could have made that case." I wasn't sure whether anyone else would have put forth the effort this case required, but I was sure glad I had!

WE'RE NOT FROM AROUND HERE

"I DIDN'T KNOW." Have you ever said that? Believe me when I tell you I've heard that a lot. The majority of the time those words were spoken by someone who was reasonably sure they were about to get a ticket. That was the case with these folks.

Although I had a heavy workload during the summer as an area wildlife biologist and later as the private lands biologist for central Alabama, I would try to get away a few times during the summer and accompany a conservation enforcement officer (CEO) checking fishermen. I always enjoyed working with CEO Jerry Fincher in Talladega County in part because we were often successful. His county had a lot of water and a lot of folks who liked to fish.

I remember one day in May of 2010 Jerry and I were checking bank fishing along the Talladega and St. Clair County line when we came upon several folks fishing from a long pier. We walked out on the pier and began checking the fishermen as we came to them. The first fellow I checked had left his license in his truck so while he went to retrieve it I checked two women sitting on the pier. Jerry moved ahead of me checking others.

It's always interesting how people respond to the presence of an officer, or should I say how they fail to respond. I would think if an officer is moving along a line of people and checking each one's fishing license, it would be a good idea to get my license out and have it ready when the officer got to me. However, it seems I may be the only person who thinks that way. Either that or I've been checking some of the most unobservant and clueless people on the planet. Oh sure, you occasionally come to the next person and they have their license out and ready but it is the exception to the norm.

Let me assure you game wardens are not the only officers who see this. I have worked many roadblocks with both county deputies and state troopers. Sometimes there would be six or eight cars in line moving toward the officers in the road. Sometimes the line moves slow. This could be because we are having people found to be in violation pull to the side of the road. However, the most common reason these lines get bogged down is the drivers having to search for their driver's license and proof of insurance. Now it would seem to me that seeing the officers in the road would prompt people to retrieve their license and insurance and have them ready when they reached the officer. Once again it, that evidently only occurs to me.

In our case, it often wasn't that these individuals were not aware they were about to be checked, they simply made no effort to retrieve their license since they hadn't bothered to obtain one! I'm sure they were hoping we would somehow pass by them, although that rarely happened.

As Jerry made his way to the last couple on the pier, they were evidently shocked to see him. I would have thought, by their reaction, we had not just checked twenty people next to them but had just popped up out of the pier beside them! He requested their license and the man immediately responded, "We didn't know, we aren't from around here!" Overhearing this I found it quite comical and watched to see how Jerry would handle it.

Jerry asked what the man meant when he said they didn't know and he replied he didn't know they needed a license because they weren't from around here. Jerry asked the obvious question, "Where are you from?" "We are from Anniston," was his reply. Well, that explained it. I mean good grief, Anniston was at least fifteen miles away in the adjacent county! Jerry looked at the man and said, "Well, you know even people from Anniston have to have a license to fish." I almost laughed out loud when the man replied, "Oh, we didn't know." They definitely know now!

How about you? We are all sometimes pretty good at saying we were not aware of something when it comes up. Folks would often either say "I didn't know" or "Since when?" upon being confronted with the fact they were breaking the law. Let me confront you with something. Jesus died for you. He took your sin and hung on a cross so you could have eternal life. All you have to do is accept Him as Savior and accept the free pardon of sin He offers. Everyone will either accept or reject Him.

You can no longer say you didn't know. Choose wisely.

HE DID WHAT?

ON A MIDSUMMER DAY, I was neck deep in wetland reserve program (WRP) monitoring. The WRP was part of the farm bill designed to reclaim wetland areas that had been degraded. Wetlands are an integral part the ecosystem. They serve as huge water filters, water storage, and habitat for many species of wildlife. The WRP was an effort to restore the hydrology of the areas that had been previously drained, often for agricultural reasons. In the restoration effort, there were many restrictions on what activities could be performed on the property. Through the farm bill administered by the USDA Natural Resource Conservation Service (NRCS), landowners received compensation for placing their property in the program.

Participation in the WRP carried with it several rules and regulations landowners had to adhere to. Part of my responsibilities as a private lands biologist in partnership with the NRCS was to monitor many of these areas in central and south Alabama to ensure compliance. I enjoyed the field visits but the corresponding paperwork not so much.

I was completing some of the paperwork after a week of property visits when I received a call from Joseph Davidson, the chief deputy with the Coosa County Sheriff's Office. The chief advised he had attempted to reach our county conservation enforcement officer but was unsuccessful. I told him the officer, the only one assigned to the county at the time, was on vacation and out of town. After a brief hesitation, the chief asked if I could possibly assist him.

He explained he was on Coosa County Road 70 in the Stewartville community serving an arrest warrant. My first thought was if he was already there then this wasn't a request to assist with the arrest of the subject, so I surmised he had run into something else. I was correct. He said the arrestee was in possession of a live raccoon and he needed to know whether or not it was legal for him to have it. This was a good question without a simple answer.

For many years the Alabama Department of Conservation and Natural Resources issued permits to individuals allowing them to keep wildlife in captivity. Although everyone knew this wasn't a good idea, the practice had been allowed forever and was therefore difficult to end. As is often the case, change doesn't come easily. It often requires a major incident to prompt the change. That was the case with the Alabama wildlife permit system.

I remember very well the events leading to the demise of the permit program. One morning I received a call from Captain Kenneth Briars, the law enforcement supervisor in the district adjacent to my county. He explained he was looking for some assistance to shut down our wildlife permit system. He and I had spoken in the past of how the program was detrimental to wildlife and a liability nightmare. I figured something must have occurred to rekindle his interest to stop the program. Boy, was I right.

Captain Briars explained they had just had an incident that once again highlighted the problems with permitting people to keep wildlife. The story was unbelievable. A resident's African lions had escaped from their confinement area and had gone to a nearby property and attacked some miniature horses. Hearing her horses in distress, the landowner responded and killed one of the lions with a .32-caliber pistol. You can't make this stuff up. Captain Briars told me he felt the time was right to dismantle the permit program. I told him I would be glad to assist him in that effort. Although I played a minor role, the captain and Supervising Wildlife Biologist Mike Sievering worked together to get the practice of permitting wildlife stopped.

    I need to point out our permit system did not include the permitting of species that were nonindigenous to Alabama. Therefore, we still have people who have lions and tigers and other exotic species in captivity. Those species do not fall under our purview. However, in most cases, citizens are no longer allowed to keep species indigenous to Alabama. While that probably doesn't lessen the number of calls from folks who have in some way acquired a raccoon or possum or whitetail fawn, it does provide us the opportunity to tell them they can either release the animal where they found it or be subject to arrest. Wildlife is meant to be in the wild. If wild animals are orphaned (which most are NOT!) that is part of nature and they should be left alone. Every year I received calls from folks who had rescued a deer fawn that was "abandoned." These folks deducted that if they saw a fawn that was not accompanied by a doe then it was obviously abandoned. They did not understand that a doe will often leave her fawn bedded and will not stay beside it all the time. In all likelihood, the doe probably witnessed the abduction of her fawn by well-meaning people who thought they were helping. I had to explain to these folks that the truth of the situation was removing fawns from the wild normally resulted in their death. I have explained in many presentations that an "orphaned" fawn could be defined as one they could catch! I have covered this topic in other stories but it is well worth repeating.

As I hope you can see the wildlife in possession situation was a complicated one. The chief deputy's question of whether or not the man could legally possess the raccoon, even with our no-wildlife-in-captivity regulations, was not a simple cut-and-dried answer. I explained to the deputy that it would depend how and where the raccoon had been acquired. Unfortunately, there are species that one would assume are indigenous but are in fact not. An aggravating and confusing situation. I told the chief I would be en route to his location.

I left my office and headed to my home, where I changed into my enforcement uniform and picked up a live trap, the only "cage" I had, and headed toward Stewartville. Upon arrival, I was met by the chief, who thanked me for coming and shared an interesting story. He told me the resident had been charged with domestic violence and knowing there were several weapons in the home the chief had accompanied the deputy who came to serve the warrant. While in the house, which was basically one room, he had observed a mounted raccoon on a shelf. As he was effecting the arrest he noticed the raccoon's head turned and followed him as he moved across the room. Not surprisingly this got the chief's attention. He asked the arrestee about the animal and he confirmed it was his pet.

I moved to the deputy's vehicle, where the man, a registered sex offender, was being held and identified myself and told him I needed to ask him a couple of questions. I removed my Miranda card from my wallet and read him the warning. He stated he understood. I asked him to tell me the story on his pet raccoon. He did not hesitate and said the raccoon had "just come up" in the yard and was covered with fire ants. He had caught the animal and removed the fire ants and had made it into a pet. He stated he had had the animal in captivity for over two years. I explained to him it was illegal to keep a wild animal and he would be charged. I also told him I would need to confiscate the animal. I asked the chief if he would accompany the man into the house to retrieve the animal. They headed toward the house.

Anytime a wild animal that was widely recognized as a rabies carrier had been in contact with humans the animal needed to be tested. I contacted the county environmentalist, whose duty it was to have the animal tested, and apprised her of the situation. She confirmed the animal would definitely need to be tested. She also asked me to interview the man concerning the interaction he and his son had had with the raccoon with an emphasis on whether either of them had been bitten by the animal.

I noticed movement toward the house and realized the defendant was coming toward me with the raccoon, a large female, riding on his shoulder. I had placed a moving blanket in the backseat of my Chevrolet Tahoe and had the large live trap on top of that. I opened the door and the man brought the coon over and, after kissing the animal, put it in the trap. He told me she was a good girl and asked that I take good care of her. I told him she would have to be tested for rabies. I did not mention that would require that she be put down.

I had thought I was going to issue the man a citation and be on my way; however, the chief stopped me with another question. He asked, "What about the turtles?" I replied, "What turtles?" He told me the guy had a whole pile of turtles and added, "I mean turtles," while holding out his arms in a big circle. I'll admit I was a little confused by the chief indicating that the man had a turtle that was two feet in diameter! I lowered the windows on my vehicle to give the caged raccoon some air and we headed toward the "turtle corral."

The turtle corral was a circular area about fifty feet across. It was lined with two-foot-tall pieces of utility poles buried in the ground side by side preventing the turtles' escape. As we neared the enclosure I spotted a "turtle" that was in fact two feet in diameter and the top of its carapace or shell was probably sixteen inches high. I wasn't sure exactly what it was but I knew it wasn't from around here! The defendant explained it was an African tortoise he had owned for fifteen years. We then spotted another tortoise that was about half the size of the first. He explained it was a Russian tortoise. While I could not confirm what the fellow was saying, neither could I dispute it. There are over thirty species of turtles in Alabama and I could identify three or four of them. To the best of my knowledge there is one indigenous tortoise and that is the gopher tortoise found in the southern part of the state. Luckily, I was familiar with the gopher tortoise and knew these were not gopher tortoises. However, as I looked around the "corral" I spotted a box turtle—an indigenous species. This was not a problem until I spotted the second box turtle. Our departmental regulations state:

> It shall be unlawful to possess more than one box turtle or to offer for sale, sell, or trade for anything of value any box turtle (Terrapene spp.), box turtle part, or reproductive product except by permit.

I asked the fellow if he held any permits allowing him to possess the turtles. He stated he did not but then explained, in great detail, how he was a turtle rescuer. He had rescued many turtles that had been hit in the road or were crossing the road where they might get hit and had brought them to his turtle sanctuary. Further investigation revealed at least twenty-five box turtles. That was twenty-four over the limit.

I must admit this was my first box turtle case in all my years of working. I told the chief deputy I needed to go ahead and take the raccoon home and prepare it for its test and I would be over to the jail shortly and handle the paperwork with the violator.

As I returned to my Tahoe I received a greeting I had partially anticipated. The pungent smell of raccoon excrement was stifling. I looked in the backseat and saw the raccoon had pulled the cargo blanket up through the bottom of the cage and shredded it and had evidently crapped several times, smearing it all around. It was a fun ride home with all the windows down and my head hanging out the window.

Arriving at home I immediately took the trap/cage out of the vehicle. Fortunately, "most" of the excrement was on the now-shredded cargo blanket. The remainder I cleaned up and then sanitized the truck and left all the doors open so it would hopefully air out.

I turned my attention to the raccoon. I thought about how sad it was that due to no fault of its own it was now going to be euthanized. It was such a waste. While human life should always trump animal life, it is sad when humans make choices that cost the animal everything. Do not misunderstand me. I have hunted most of my life and have killed many animals. I am a certified wildlife biologist by the Wildlife Society and worked thirty years managing wildlife habitat. I believe fully man has been given dominion over wildlife. However, the problem here is folks want all of their rights and privileges without accepting any of the responsibilities that go with those rights and privileges. Before some folks go berserk, thinking the fellow in this story was simply a Good Samaritan being picked on by heavy-handed law enforcement, I would say when your illegal "help" causes animals to have to be put down, it isn't much help. There are right ways to do things. I digress...

I completed the unenviable task of dispatching the raccoon. Unfortunately, an animal that will be tested for rabies should not be shot in the head to avoid damaging the brain stem needed for the testing. Therefore, it takes a little longer to dispatch the animal. With that duty complete I headed to the jail.

En route to the jail I contacted a member of our covert squad. The undercover unit normally handled turtle cases and I wanted to let them know what was going on. When I told him about seizing the raccoon, he immediately asked if I had had the defendant sign a release form. I told him I had not and that I didn't know such a form existed. He assured me I needed to have the fellow sign a form and said he would bring one to the jail if need be. I told him I was en route to the jail to complete the paperwork on the arrest for having the raccoon. He again became excited and asked if I had not arrested the man at the site of the violation. I told him I had advised the man he was under arrest and told him I would handle his paperwork at the jail. The covert officer informed me I could not do that. This sort of took me by surprise. I told him I could do that and I was on my way to do it now. He again stated I had to arrest him at the scene of the offense and I countered that was not the case. I understood he worked a lot more difficult cases than I did and with a lot of different judges. However, he needed to understand I had worked with my judge and circuit clerk for many years and hundreds of cases and I understood what would and would not work. He did bring the seizure form, which was also a release of liability, to the jail. When I advised him about the turtles, he asked if I knew that each turtle over the one allowed would be a separate case and I told him I did but felt it would be best if he handled those violations. He said he would talk with his cohort who normally handled turtle cases.

    I had the prisoner brought to a holding cell where I interviewed him concerning the raccoon and the turtles. I learned some interesting information. I had him sign the seizure form and allowed him to sign a bond for possession of a protected live animal seeing how he was already incarcerated on the domestic violence charge.

The next month the cases were on the district court docket. When the subject's name was called he approached the judge's bench. The judge advised him of his charges and asked if he had an attorney or if he needed the court to appoint him one. He requested that a lawyer be appointed and the judge gave him the Appointment of Legal Counsel Due to Hardship form and instructed him to complete it.

Shortly thereafter he returned the form and after scanning it the judge appointed an attorney for the cases. The appointed attorneys would normally receive numerous appointments each court date so it took a while for them to get around to all the cases.

Eventually the attorney caught the assistant district attorney (ADA) and they went to the jury room to confer about the case. Shortly after that the ADA came to the courtroom door and motioned for me to come and join the discussion. I sat down across the table from the defense attorney and he explained that since the fellow was facing the domestic violence charge and was going to enter into a plea agreement on it they would move that the raccoon in captivity case be dismissed. This was always the view of the defense attorneys. If there was some other "significant" case involved the trivial wildlife case should be dropped. That was one reason I definitely wasn't their favorite since I never agreed to that. I held firm in this case as well and told the counselor I felt the man should be found guilty since he obviously was guilty. Of course, this did not fit with the attorney's planned agreement. He looked at the ADA with a disgusted "help me here" look. I had worked with the ADA for many years and he knew how I felt about every case I brought to court. My viewpoint was if they weren't guilty, I wouldn't have arrested them. In an attempt at justification the defense attorney said it was his understanding the man had kept the raccoon as a pet and he didn't think that was a bad thing. He then added, "It's not like he hurt the animal." This was my opening and I quickly replied, "In my opinion, someone grinding a raccoon's teeth off with a Dremel tool was hurting the animal!" The ADA immediately said, "He did what?" I knew I now had their attention. I explained how when I asked if the raccoon had bitten the man or his son he had replied it had. He continued, saying that was why he had ground the animal's teeth off using an electric rotary tool. I checked the animal's mouth and sure enough, the teeth had been ground down smooth. I went on to say I felt this actually constituted "a take" seeing how the animal could not be returned to the wild. I concluded by saying the man's actions had ultimately resulted in the death of the animal since it had to be put down to be tested for rabies. I looked at the ADA and he looked at the defense counsel and said, "He's going to have to plead guilty to this and pay a fine." We agreed on a $250 fine and court costs for a total of $499. While it wouldn't bring the animal back, I hoped it would make the man think before taking another animal into captivity.

As for the turtle cases, I contacted our local officer when he returned from vacation and gave him a rundown of what had occurred. I asked if he would get with the covert unit and handle the turtle violations. I never heard any more about it, which wasn't unusual for covert cases.

Even with the regulations prohibiting the holding of wildlife in captivity, it still continues to be a problem. Many people who capture wildlife have good intentions. Unfortunately, they often go about things in the wrong way.

For over thirty-six years I have dealt with a lot of folks who have attempted to domesticate a wild animal. In addition, I have heard of hundreds of situations that have occurred in Alabama and I know it's no different in other states. Whether it's a deer fawn, squirrel, raccoon, snake, bird, or whatever, these situations almost always turn out badly for the animal. I understand that many people are well intentioned and think they are doing the right thing. Unfortunately, they are normally wrong. I and probably every officer in the state have been forced to euthanize an animal someone has tried to fashion into a pet. This puts the officer in an untenable position. Many officers have had to endure unwarranted abuse, ridicule, and slander because of someone else's bad decision. That's not to mention the many people who have had to undergo the painful treatment for rabies after being exposed to an infected wild "pet."

If I didn't love wildlife, I would not have been in this profession. I can definitely understand the allure of having a wild animal as a pet. However, as I have told many people who have "rescued" an "orphaned" deer fawn or "saved" a raccoon, squirrel, or bird that has fallen out of a tree, it is best to let nature take its course. Wild animals are meant to be wild. Do them a favor and leave them in the wild.

RAINBOW PEOPLE

As I have stated numerous times there was no shortage of crazy things that occurred in the wild. Of course, not nearly as many of those incidents involved wildlife as they did people. One stressful aspect of being on a wildlife management area (WMA) was the fact that most of our WMAs were privately owned. While we did lease the hunting rights, we did not pay anything to the landowner other than in-kind services. Those services were primarily related to maintaining access on the WMA. That included installing and maintaining culverts under the road, grading roads, dozer work, and even building bridges. Although those services were worth a lot of money, the lease contained a clause that would allow the landowner to cancel our lease with only a ninety-day notice. Early on, long-term leases were the norm; however, as time went by the lease terms shortened until many were down to a year-by-year basis.

On the other hand, several of our WMAs were located in national forests. These areas were viewed as secure. Although managers on these areas had job security, dealing with the federal government had its drawbacks. I'll give you a minute to try to comprehend that dealing with the government could be troublesome! The forest service was constantly being sued by various groups who wanted their agenda pushed forward. They were either being sued for cutting timber or failing to cut timber or to allow them to use prescribed fire or to stop them from using prescribed fire. It got to the point where you had to have a public hearing to decide whether or not we could plant a food plot on the area. If this wasn't enough of a headache, since this was federal land we had to allow the public to access it freely. Now while I believe the public should be able to utilize our national forests, it carries with it some real problems. One of the problems we faced from time to time was the Rainbow people.

Research tells me the Rainbow Family was founded in the late '60s. Since 1972 they have held annual "gatherings" in national forests across the country. While most of these gatherings occur in July, some Rainbows would show up throughout the year. The gatherings were supposed to exhibit the ideals of peace, love, freedom, harmony, and community. However, in my experience the Rainbows would normally place a heavy burden on the counties where they gathered. They would typically overwhelm the local health department by demanding services and would leave a considerable impact on the ground.

Unfortunately, for my coworker, wildlife biologist Gene Carver, the Rainbows decided the Hollins Wildlife Management Area in ultra-rural Clay County would be a good place for a gathering. While, as I mentioned, the "official" gatherings took place in July, we would also have Rainbows at other times of the year and some even coincided with hunting season, which caused some conflicts. One problem was the Rainbows would totally take over a campground, not leaving any area for hunters or anyone else to camp. Since most of our hunters were local folks, this wasn't a tremendous problem. However, there were other problems.

I remember Gene relating to me the conversation he had with a WMA bow hunter who had an incident to remember. Gene said he knew this was going to be good when the fellow began by saying, "Gene, you ain't gonna believe this!" He described the fellow as being wild-eyed and visibly shaken. The man said, "I was up in my tree stand overlooking a good deer trail when I heard something running in the leaves. I got my bow ready and was watching in the direction of the noise. All of a sudden, I saw something coming over the hill, and Gene," at this point the man stopped talking and looked all around to make sure no one else was listening and then continued, saying, "it was a red-headed woman and she was naked as a jaybird!" The man then watched Gene intently to gauge his reaction. Gene said he fought to keep a straight face and the man continued. "Gene, she was laughing and giggling and ran right past my tree." The man's voice grew in pitch as he related the details. "Then I heard something else coming." He again warned, "Gene, you ain't gonna believe this," and he then blurted out, "It was two naked men and they came running along right behind her. I didn't know what to do!" The man then said, "Now Gene, that's the honest truth." Although the urge to tease the man was strong, Gene said he could tell this fellow had been traumatized enough. He told the man he believed the story and explained the Rainbows were in town.

The Choccolocco Wildlife Management Area in Calhoun and Cleburne Counties was another favorite spot for the Rainbow crowd. As you can imagine this would often cause quite a stir in rural east central Alabama. What was to me a humorous incident occurred when a local game warden approached a group of Rainbows. Believe me when I tell you this officer was one of a kind. Although he has long been retired and passed away a couple of years ago, his exploits are still legendary. One of the Rainbow women asked the officer, "Do you have to have a fishing license if you are on welfare?" The officer answered the question with a very simple "No." This wasn't the officer's first rodeo and he was well known locally for being a "sight," as people around here say. The woman promptly retrieved her rod and reel and cast her lure into the stream. The officer instantly walked over to her and asked to see her fishing license. She immediately protested and said she had just asked him whether or not she had to have a fishing license and he had said no. The officer replied, "You asked if you had to have a fishing license if you were on welfare." "That's right," she scoffed. "Well, to the best of my knowledge there is no requirement that a person on welfare has to have a fishing license, but you do have to have one if you want to fish!" I miss you, Don.

You can't make this stuff up.

SHOTS FIRED—AT US!

How many folks do you know who go out into the middle of nowhere, in the dark of night, hoping to encounter some armed individual, who possesses poor judgment, few morals, and no respect for the law or the wildlife resource? You know, when you put it that way it doesn't really sound like a smart thing to do. However, I have spent countless nights hoping just such an individual would pass my location and afford me the opportunity to apprehend them.

The individuals described above are what we commonly refer to as night hunters. These are folks who unscrupulously ride the roads or sit in shooting houses after dark in areas where deer are known to frequent (all of Alabama) and attempt to kill those deer normally with a high-powered rifle under the cover of darkness. These people have no idea what may be beyond their target. Yet they have no qualms about unleashing a projectile traveling three thousand feet per second into the darkness. In my experience, these bullets have found houses, vehicles, farm equipment, and livestock. Some nighttime deer hunters will not hesitate to shoot at a deer no matter where it is. I've had deer shot in front yards, backyards, pastures, hayfields, and under security lights in the country and in the city limits!

Working night hunting can be extremely boring; it can also be deadly. When I began my career, one of my mentors, Conservation Enforcement Officer (CEO) Hershel Patterson, shared with me how his former partner had been shot and killed by night hunters. That's pretty sobering. Yet protecting the resource and the public by attempting to apprehend the violators is a major part of the job during the deer season. I have spent many nights in the middle of nowhere without seeing a vehicle or hearing a shot all night. Therefore, when working night hunting we always hoped someone would either shoot near our location or at least shine a light in a field in front of us.

It had been a long deer season and there was still three weeks until it would end. The violations didn't stop just because the deer season ended; however, they normally did taper off significantly. Talladega County CEO Jerry Fincher and I had worked many long hours without catching a night hunter. I was actually beginning to think I must be bad luck seeing how Jerry had made several night hunting cases working alone but we had yet to catch one together this year. I must admit I receive great gratification each time Jerry makes a good case since he routinely refers to me as his unofficial field training officer (FTO). When he went to work we did not have a formal FTO program as we do today. Therefore, I in effect trained him. He turned out to be an excellent student. He was recently promoted to lieutenant.

We decided to work a major roadway in Talladega County that normally had deer standing in the fields. As I always reminded Jerry, working night hunting isn't rocket science. You simply go to where the deer are. Even if you caught someone there last night, go back. We got set up around 9:00 p.m. and the traffic seemed to totally dry up. Jerry had suffered from a stomach ailment all winter and sleep for him had been hard to come by. I told him to try to rest and I would keep vigil. He finally closed his eyes and I watched the road.

Marine Police Captain Michael Patrick had come to assist us and had taken up a position about a mile from ours on the same roadway. Although he was in the Marine Police Division with his primary responsibility enforcing boating rules and regulations, Captain Patrick had plenty of experience working night hunting. Seeing how during the winter boaters were few and far between, many marine police officers would assist CEOs in problem areas. When you had the night hunting problems we did, assistance was greatly appreciated.

The road where we were set up was a familiar one. Jerry had made many cases there. The high number of deer standing in the crop fields along the highway was more temptation than many folks could endure. We hoped tonight would once again prove to be good for us and bad for the violators.

Things were really slow until about midnight. I finally caught sight of some headlights that appeared to be moving slowly. A slow roller at midnight was usually a good prospect. I observed as the pickup eased along the road moving right to left and soon came to a stop, less than one hundred yards from our location. When a spotlight illuminated the field, I nudged Jerry and he replied, "I see it." I realized Jerry was honing a skill I too had developed over time. This skill, the ability to sleep while at the same time hear and see, is a great asset to a game warden. I know it sounds unbelievable but it can be done.

Not spotting anything in the field, the light went off and the truck eased down the road. We called Captain Patrick and told him we had one shining and they were headed toward his location. The vehicle disappeared over a small rise in the road and we pulled out behind them. When we topped the rise, the truck had stopped and the passenger was once again illuminating a field with the handheld spotlight. Once the driver saw our headlights, he put the pedal to the metal and took off at a high rate of speed.

Years earlier, the driver would not have seen our headlights seeing how we would not have had them on. For many years driving without any headlights was a common practice for game wardens. It was a tactic that often worked well. Granted it wasn't the safest thing to do and for that reason our department adopted a policy outlawing the practice.

Fortunately, we had got the jump on these poachers and closed the distance between us before they could get up to speed. We activated our blue lights and radioed Captain Patrick telling him the vehicle was coming his way and didn't appear to be planning on stopping.

Speeds continued to rise as we neared the captain's position. As the vehicle passed his hiding spot, he put his thirty plus years of experience to work and with perfect timing he came out immediately behind the vehicle. The captain was driving a Chevy Tahoe and it would run. Evidently the second unit arriving on the scene motivated the driver to give it up and he applied the brakes and slid to a stop in the roadway. It was not unusual for the people we blue lighted to stop in the middle of the road instead of pulling to the right side. I'm not sure why that was but it happened that way as often as not. While that wasn't uncommon what happened next was a first for me.

Before the truck stopped moving, the passenger jumped from the truck, rifle in hand, and ran through the ditch into a dense pine thicket. We slid to a stop and exited our vehicle. Captain Patrick went to the driver's side of the violator's truck while Jerry and I turned our attention to the woods and the fleeing armed subject. As I entered the ditch, I could hear the man crashing through the trees not twenty yards in front of me. In over twenty-three years and 160 night hunting arrests, I had never had this happen and was somewhat unsure about how exactly to proceed. Just then a shot rang out! This development quickly helped me decide what to do. I immediately gave up the pursuit and took cover on the other side of our vehicle. Jerry was right beside me. We stared at each other with an uneasy look of disbelief that asked, Can you believe that? We did not know for sure whether or not we had just been shot at but we were confident about where our shots would go in the event we saw a muzzle flash. Fortunately, that didn't happen. It is an uncomfortable feeling knowing there is an armed violator in the woods where he can't be seen and you are on the road that is illuminated with blue and white lights. We heard a little more rustling in the woods and then all was quiet.

Captain Patrick had removed the driver of the pickup and had him handcuffed and lying face down on the cold pavement. We stayed behind cover and moved to the driver. We obtained his name and recognized he shared the same name as a police officer in a nearby jurisdiction. I asked if the officer was his father and he said he was. We asked who his passenger was and he claimed he did not know. We asked more *emphatically* and he told us he had met the guy standing in front of a local convenience store and he had said he would like to go hunting. I asked if he realized what a stupid story that was and didn't get an answer.

Our intensity was high and we again asked the man for the identity of his accomplice and he again said he had met him at the store. I asked whose gun the man had been using and he said he had brought his own gun. I replied, "So a guy was standing in front of the Quik Mart holding a rifle and saying he wanted to go night hunting and you picked him up?" I hoped pointing out the idiocy of his story might shake his tongue loose. It didn't. Getting nowhere fast, Jerry asked the man if his dad's number was in his phone and he said it was. Jerry called the father, apprised him of the situation, and asked who he thought would be with his son. He replied it would be one of two guys. We asked our subject which one it was and he gave us the name. Jerry called the man's name into the night but got no response. We told the man he needed to call his friend on the phone. He was uncuffed and given his phone.

Let's set this up. While out on a totally illegal night hunting escapade you have just been chased by the game warden. You jumped out of the still moving vehicle carrying a high-powered rifle. With two game wardens in pursuit and yelling for you to stop you fire off a round from the rifle. You continue to run through the darkness and your phone rings and you stop and answer it. I would like to say I was shocked, but I wasn't. Young folks today are helpless without their phone. They literally view it as their lifeline.

The driver told the runner we had him in custody and he needed to come on out. I could hear as the man responded he didn't know what to do. I took the phone and spoke to the subject. I identified myself and told him he needed to come out NOW! He said he was scared and didn't know what to do. I replied he had every reason to be scared and if he didn't want things to get a lot scarier he needed to put his gun down and come out with his hands above his head. He said he no longer had his rifle and didn't have a clue where it was or where he was. I asked if he could see our blue lights and he said he could not. I asked what he could see and he replied he could see a security light. I told him to walk to the light with his hands raised above his head.

Units from both the Childersburg Police Department and the Talladega Sheriff's Office had arrived to assist us and we asked them to go down the road and watch for the man walking out to the light we could see south of the road. They took him into custody without incident.

Both suspects were transported to the Talladega County Jail. We charged the men with hunting at night, hunting from the public road, hunting by aid of a vehicle, and hunting without a permit. After a long discussion with the assistant district attorney, the subject who had fired the rifle was charged with reckless endangerment. After about four hours of paperwork we were on our way home at 5:00 a.m.

Both individuals pled guilty in open court and received fines totaling over $8,000. I'm sure you may be thinking that got their attention and I hope it did. However, I will tell you the driver told us on the scene that we had caught his cousin two weeks earlier!

What does it take to get your attention? By the grace of God, I had previously survived several close calls. After this I had yet another one to praise Him for, and I do! While this incident was scarier than most, the truth is tomorrow isn't guaranteed for any of us. Life is fragile and may be short. As I edit this story, during the last two months I have been diagnosed with cancer, have undergone surgery, and have had a port placed in my chest so I can receive immunotherapy. None of that was on my bucket list! But, it's life. It makes it a lot easier to face the future knowing who holds it and where I will spend eternity. Choose Jesus. It makes all the difference.

NEAR NAKED POCKET BAITER

IF YOU HAVE NEVER CALLED IN a gobbling turkey on a cool spring morning you have missed out one of God's most awesome scenes. Although the bird's brain is the size of an acorn, his wariness coupled with unbelievable eyesight makes him a true challenge. I have been blessed to live in a turkey-rich area and have spent a lot of time hunting the birds there and across the country. Therefore, you might guess when I received word of someone violating the turkey laws, I didn't take it very well.

One cool spring morning, I received a call from Conservation Enforcement Officer (CEO) Earl Brown asking me to assist him with checking a property that was baited for turkey. I had utter disdain for anyone who would stoop so low as to shoot a turkey over bait so I was more than ready to go. Earl came by my house and we drove to a property in the Ray community of Coosa County. The officer told me this guy was a perpetual violator and needed to be caught. He said the area was baited with cracked corn, which I had learned was indicative of older baiters.

We split up and eased into the property. Working turkey hunting is inherently dangerous in that your quarry is in all likelihood wearing full camo and has the advantage of already being in the area and sitting still. By contrast you are moving through the area trying to find the equivalent of a needle in a haystack. When you add the illegal element of the area being baited, you raise the stakes even more.

Within a few minutes I heard Earl whistle, indicating he had found his target. When I arrived, Earl had the guy sitting on the ground in front of our truck. He asked me to start the paperwork on the guy while he went to gather a sample of the bait.

I asked the man for his driver's license. As he handed me the license, he asked, "What's this all about?" Although I felt certain Earl had informed him of the problem, I told him I was going to issue him a citation for hunting over bait. Little did I know this was going to trigger a show unlike any I had ever witnessed.

When I told the fellow he was under arrest for hunting over bait he began to visibly shake and say, "No." He repeatedly stated, "I don't have any bait." By this time, I had arrested a lot of folks and several of them had gotten very upset about it. However, this was definitely something new and different! As I watched he began taking off his camo jacket. I wasn't sure if he was getting ready to fight or was just starting to sweat from the anxiety. After getting out of the jacket, he turned all the pockets wrong side out and held it where I could see. After throwing the coat on the ground, he began removing his shirt. This was long before body cameras were ever thought about which is too bad seeing how it would have been an interesting video. Not only would what he was doing been something to see, I'm certain the look on my face would have been hilarious as I was somewhat dumbfounded! Regaining some of my composure, I told the man there was no need for him to undress. He replied, "I don't have any bait." He sat down on the ground and removed his shoes and socks. Not sure how far this was going to go, I hollered for Earl to come to my location. The man was now sitting on the ground with no shirt, no shoes, and no socks. He looked up at me and again said, "I don't have any bait." I told him I had not said he was baited; I had said he was hunting over bait.

Soon Earl arrived and seeing the partially dressed man on the ground looked at me with another look I wish I had on video! His face begged the question, What have you done to this guy? I told him when I placed the man under arrest he started saying he didn't have bait and began taking his clothes off. Earl looked at the man and held up a ziplock bag containing cracked corn and said, "He doesn't have any now, he had already put it out." This was when I learned a lesson about baiting turkeys.

While many outlaws would scatter feed all over creation, others would carry a small amount, a pocketful, of cracked corn or wheat into the woods with them each day. They would normally scatter the feed in the area before they departed. Turkeys would soon find the feed and would frequent the area. By using the small amount, theoretically the turkeys would eat all of the feed every day, thereby removing any evidence on the small chance the game warden might come along. We called these outlaws *pocket baiters*. This system was effective; however, it did not take a lot of times in the woods to be able recognize where baiting was taking place. Once turkeys located the morsels, the leaves in the area would soon look as though someone had been through with a rototiller.

Although this man was arrested for hunting by the aid of bait, I do not know whether or not he had been caught with bait in his pocket in the past, but I can verify he did not have anything in his pockets or up his sleeve that day! During my career I had a lot of people try a lot of different things in an attempt to get out of a ticket but that was the only stripper I remember.

WAIT A MINUTE, JACK

ONE THING I FEEL CERTAIN all law enforcement officers deal with at one time or another is trying to communicate with a subject or multiple subjects who speak another language. Notice I didn't say who can't speak English since, in my experience, many who act as if they cannot speak English actually can.

Early in my career I would, on occasion, encounter Vietnamese people hunting on the wildlife management area. These folks were generally affable. However, the only English word many of them knew was evidently "No." Many times, I encountered them with their firearm in their hand and I would approach and ask what they were hunting and they would reply, "No." When this occurred I would quickly resort to the age-old technique of speaking louder. Although this doesn't help anything, it is still the first tool that comes out of the pouch. When I would remember that tool normally never worked, I would go to the next technique, the hand gesture. I would loudly say "hunting" and hold up my imaginary rifle and pretend to shoot. This would normally get an affirmative head nod and sometimes they would pull a squirrel or rabbit from their pocket.

You may have noticed earlier when I said I would attempt to ask what they were hunting—this was a necessary question because you never knew. I learned early on some folks were quite the opportunists. While one member of a party might have a couple of squirrels another might have a blue jay. Some folks didn't cull anything. I had no doubt they were eating everything they took so I cut them some slack most of the time. Someone who would pick up a road-killed possum to take home and eat had enough problems without me hassling them!

Later in my career officers began to encounter more and more Hispanic individuals. An officer in a nearby county explained to me an interesting contact he and his partner had with a group of fishermen on the creek bank. The two officers had split up with one going north and the other south along the creek. The officer on the upper side ran into problems almost immediately. He encountered a Hispanic family group with several lines in the water. He approached who he assumed was the father and asked for the man's fishing license. The man responded in broken English and with a hand gesture of outstretched arms with his palms up. It was obvious he was saying he didn't understand. The officer turned to the woman and got the same response. One technique which very often proved successful was to go to the children. Many of these young children would be fluent in English and Spanish and therefore could serve as a good interpreter. In addition the children would normally tell you the truth. Unfortunately when our officer approached these kids, a stern look from their parents rendered them mute.

Frustrated, the officer went back down the creek bank and found the other officer and told him he had a problem with a bunch of folks that couldn't speak English. To which the partner replied, "They can speak English, you just have to know how to talk to them." "Then why don't you come and show me?" was his quick retort.

The two officers made their way back to the group and the second officer went to the father and asked to see his fishing license. The man again raised his hands in front of him and indicated he didn't understand. The officer made a casting motion and acted as if he was holding a piece of paper and said loudly, "fishing license." He again got the same response. Not giving up the officer made a motion as if he was turning a steering wheel and loudly said, "driving license." He again received the hands-up-no-comprende response.

Becoming somewhat frustrated the officer quickly devised a plan. He eased his hand behind his back and removed his handcuffs from the pouch. Keeping his arm hidden he got a cuff in his hand and again asked the man for his license. Once again the man gestured with his hands and when he did the officer quickly slapped a cuff onto his wrist. Immediately, in clear English, the man said, "Wait a minute, Jack." To this the first officer responded, "You can speak English you son of a gun." The wife replied in clear English, "You can't call him a son of a gun!" Incredulous, the officer said, "You can all speak English!"

After this quick exchange, the handcuffed man asked the officer what he needed to see. Believe it or not, the man had a valid fishing license. Evidently the whole exchange had been intended to frustrate the officers. I can't remember for sure how they said the encounter ended, but I seem to recall something about the fellow receiving a ticket for fishing by the aid of bait or something I couldn't comprehend!

Fast forward several years and I am working a large detail below a hydroelectric dam. At this time the number of illegal aliens had mushroomed and on any given day you could encounter hundreds of folks fishing below the dams in the Coosa River system. Our lieutenant had put together all of the officers in the south end of the district to address the numerous complaints coming from the folks fishing at the dams. The complaints ran from taking over the limit to keeping undersized fish to illegally taking fish by snagging and using nets.

With spotters in place informing us as to what was happening, we would move into the area and begin checking licenses and for other violations. The detail was extremely successful.

Once again there was often a language barrier. As I checked a middle-aged man fishing from a platform I requested his fishing license. In broken English he told me he had a license but did not have it with him. I requested his personal information and he provided me with an international identification card. It was always interesting to view one of these identification cards. The card would normally have a lot of insignia from some foreign country on it but would it have an address from Alabama? I ran his information through our dispatch to see whether or not he actually did have a license. The dispatcher soon informed me there was no record of him having a fishing license. I returned to him and told him our records did not show him as having a license. That did not receive much of a response. I advised him I was going to issue him a ticket for fishing without a license. I took out my bond book and begin filling out the required information. One of the blanks asked for the individual's occupation or employer. Despite the fact the ID card said the man lived in Bessemer, I asked, "Where do you live?" and he responded, "Bessemer." I asked, "What do you do there?" and with a bit of a curious look on his face he replied, "Live." As I looked at the man a grin spread across my face and I said, "I guess I walked right into that one, didn't I?" Then a grin came across his face. I realized he too understood much more English than I did Spanish. I finished the paperwork and explained the procedure to him.

The entire time I had been dealing with the man, there were two younger fellows on the rocks below feverishly casting into the river. I directed my attention to these individuals and asked to see their fishing licenses. Both young men immediately told me they did not have a license. However, they quickly added they weren't keeping any fish they were just fishing for fun. I explained a fishing license was required to fish whether you caught any fish or not. It was obvious both young men knew their weak attempt at a defense was in fact very weak. I asked for their driver's licenses and they both produced licenses which showed they lived locally. As I wrote the tickets, I noticed the one fellow had a somewhat strange sounding name and I asked where he was from and he responded "Kazakhstan." I must admit I didn't see that one coming! Once again you never knew what was coming next when you worked with game and fish!

NOBODY LIKES A SMART ALECK

PEOPLE KNOW CONSERVATION ENFORCEMENT OFFICERS (CEOs) are out and about during the deer season. In fact, many folks think that is the only time CEOs work. Of course, that is far from the truth. Yes, the deer season is a very active time and in Alabama it spans four months. Preparation for working deer season starts long before opening day just as for many other seasons. That's not to mention the myriad of other calls that come in. There was plenty of work to go around.

Since our regulation concerning hunting by the aid of bait stated it was illegal to hunt any area where feeding had taken place until all the feed had been removed or consumed for at least ten days prior to hunting, we would often return to known baited areas during the ten days prior to opening day of the season. This way, any area we found containing feed would be considered baited for opening day. This did not mean we would automatically arrest anyone hunting in such an area but it did give us that option. Obviously, this was before the state legislature passed the law allowing people to hunt by the aid of bait if they purchased a bait privilege license.

Two days prior to the opening day of the gun deer season several years ago I accompanied CEOs Jerry Fincher and Greg

Gilliland checking a property in north Talladega County. Almost immediately upon entering the property we started finding corn. Eventually we located three tree stands with corn on the ground beneath them. While folks will use anything you can think of to bait deer, corn was by far the most common. Like these folks, many people would simply pour out a bag of corn in a pile in front of their stand to afford them an easy shot if deer came to the bait. While some people kept it simple, others would utilize some type of feeder. This could be anything from a fifty-five-gallon drum cut in half to a five-gallon bucket to a two-liter Coke bottle. It might be a piece of PVC pipe tied to a tree or a huge tripod feeder capable of holding five hundred pounds of corn. No matter what the delivery method, if the person was sitting and looking at the feed in an effort to take an animal they were in violation.

Two days later, the opening morning of gun deer season, we again checked the property. As we approached the first baited location, we encountered a husband and wife in the tree stand. We instructed them to exit the stand. We escorted them across the field they had been watching to a spot under another stand where there had been a large pile of corn. The majority of the corn had been removed though a remnant remained. I remained there talking with the couple while Officers Gilliland and Fincher went to the next stand approximately a hundred yards away. In speaking with the pair, I learned this was their first time to be on the property. They stated they had been put in the stand by their daughter's boyfriend, Johnathan, and they had no knowledge of feeding having taken place on the property. I had no real reason not to believe them; however, I had been lied to many times before.

A couple of minutes later, I spotted the officers headed our way with a young fellow, who I assumed was Johnathan, in tow. The young fellow appeared to be about twenty years old and even at a distance I could tell he was in a bad mood. Although we had not called attention to it, we were standing where the corn had been just two days earlier. In a belligerent tone he stated, "I know y'all have been trespassing on this property and my dad cleaned up the corn yesterday." I immediately recognized that his spontaneous exclamation just might come back to haunt him. I asked him if the other two people there knew anything about the corn and he stated they did not. He belligerently stated it did not make any difference since his dad had removed the corn the previous day.

Our young obstinate friend unfortunately did not understand the hunting laws and regulations as well as he thought. He evidently believed since the bait had been removed, anyone hunting there would no longer be in violation. This was not true. Obviously, he was not familiar with the regulation that stated all bait must be removed ten days prior to hunting.

Since the couple claimed this was their first time on the property, they had no knowledge of any corn having been in the area, and the fact their "guide" had placed them in the stand and told us they were not aware of any bait having been there, we did not arrest them.

They had a good attitude and thanked us for understanding their situation. They had been cordial throughout the whole ordeal. Their guide was, however, on the other end of the spectrum. Any time anyone tells an officer they don't have the authority to write them a ticket, it provides the officer with a great opportunity to prove them wrong! Based on his repeated acknowledgment that the corn had been removed the previous day and the fact he was hunting deer on the property with a high-powered rifle overlooking an area where the corn had been, we decided he should be arrested.

To my way of thinking, this was a great example of using proper discretion. The judge saw it the same way.

Many people think much like the young fellow in this story in that if they try to rectify a situation, all is good. While it is admirable to try to right a wrong, if a wrong has been committed there are consequences.

That reminds me of another case where we arrested two young guys for hunting without a permit. It was pretty cut-and-dried in that they were on property where they had no permission to be with rifles in hand and readily admitted they were deer hunting. However, when they appeared in court they brought their uncle with them to plead their case. He was not an attorney; however, when the judge asked how they pled, the uncle blurted out their defense. He said, "Well they didn't even shoot anything." The judge held his composure although I could tell he was ready to explode. He definitely did not appreciate outbursts in his court and especially not from someone who wasn't even involved in the case. The judge asked me for the facts in the case and quickly found the pair guilty.

Many times, people take a "no harm, no foul" attitude. Many feel that unless an animal is taken, no crime has been committed. This is obviously not true. Many folks will tell you that it isn't against the law if they don't get caught. That too is not true and is in fact a very dangerous philosophy.

People who think they have gotten by with something can lure themselves into a false sense of security. Sin is sin whether you get caught or not and the truth is you are caught every time. The Lord knows and sees everything. One of the most powerful verses in the Bible is found in Galatians and it says God is not mocked. You will reap what you sow. That's pretty easy to understand.

The people in these cases didn't think they had done anything wrong. They were mistaken. Sin has consequences; however, forgiveness is available. You can seek it today. Tomorrow may be eternally too late!

MAKE BAG PUT CRAP IN

WORKING WITH THE HUNTING PUBLIC gave me many opportunities to view people from various cultures. Although one of the predominant cultures was redneck, there were other interesting characters out there as well. One group I had previously had very little exposure to was the Vietnamese. I must admit I did not think that would change when I moved to ultra-rural Coosa County.

The Coosa Wildlife Management Area (WMA) was forty-five miles north of Montgomery and we often had Vietnamese hunters from the capital city on the WMA. I rarely had trouble with these people other than the fact they always answered every question with "No." "Have you had any luck today?" "No." "Did you kill anything?" "No." Although they always answered no, it was not at all unusual to find evidence that spoke to the contrary such as a squirrel lying in the floorboard of their vehicle. The language barrier was a problem and I eventually learned to communicate with hand gestures and they learned to show me their license and permit. There were usually relatively few problems.

One evening I was checking vehicles just below our equipment shed on the main road that traversed the WMA. My dual role of wildlife area manager and conservation enforcement officer often dictated I work most of the day on projects on the

WMA and then work law enforcement in the evening when hunters were leaving the area.

Just before dusk, I sat up just below the WMA shop at an intersection of two of the major roads on the area. At dusk, I stepped out into the road as a pickup neared my location. I flagged the truck to a stop and realized it was being driven by a lone Vietnamese man. I estimated him to be maybe fifty years old. I walked to the window of his pickup and asked to see his license and permit. He produced the documents and I asked to see the rifle that was lying in the passenger's seat. It was a violation to carry a loaded weapon in a vehicle on the WMA and we strictly enforced the rule due to the safety hazard posed by a loaded gun in a vehicle. I checked the rifle and found it to be unloaded. I asked the driver if he had any other weapons in the vehicle and he shook his head indicating he did not. I inquired as to whether he had been successful hunting and he again shook his head negatively.

Having been working in law enforcement for a few years, I had developed something of a sixth sense that would sometimes (unfortunately not always) kick in and prompt me to look a little further. I was getting that feeling and I asked the man to step out of his vehicle. The fellow stepped out and I motioned for him to move to the front of the vehicle. Keeping one eye on the man, I proceeded to look through the truck. We were fortunate that soon after the wildlife management system was developed the state legislature had passed a law giving us the authority to search any vehicle and/or person on the WMA. I reached under the driver's seat and felt the unmistakable grip of a handgun. I pulled the .357 magnum out from under the seat and found it to be fully loaded. I unloaded the weapon and held it up for the man to see and had to bite my lip to keep from laughing when he indicated it was his by pointing to himself. I completed the search of the truck and decided I would issue him a citation for the loaded firearm. He was actually in violation of at least two management area regulations. The pistol was not a legal firearm for hunting on the WMA, and it was loaded in the vehicle. In addition, he did not possess a pistol permit, which meant he was in violation of the concealed carry law.

I advised him I was going to issue him a ticket and I needed his driver's license. He gave me the license and I escorted him over and had him sit in the passenger seat of my truck while I handled the paperwork for the loaded gun. His driver's license had all of the pertinent information I needed with the exception of his place of employment. Up until this point, we had communicated primarily through hand gestures and head nods but now I needed to know where the man worked. He understood my question fairly easily. Me trying to understand his answer was a whole different thing.

When I asked where he worked he immediately responded by saying what sounded to me like "Werwa." I indicated I did not understand by shrugging my shoulders and again held my hands up in the "I don't understand" gesture. He understood and again slowly said "Werwa." I had absolutely no clue what the man was trying to say. I again indicated I did not understand and he again very slowly said "Werwa." I was at a loss as to how to decipher what the man was saying. I sat for a moment and had an idea. I asked, "What do you do?" In his best broken English, he uttered, "Make plastic bag—put crap in." Although I felt I understood what he had said, I realized I was getting nowhere fast! I repeated to him, "You make plastic bags to put crap in?" and he immediately began smiling and shaking his head yes. Well now I knew what he did, but I had no idea where he did it. As I sat wondering whether or not just to write "crap bag maker" on the occupation line of the ticket, the man suddenly jumped out of the truck and ran toward his vehicle. Although startled at first, I quickly realized he must have thought of something that might bridge this communication gap. Sure enough the man came running back and, in his hand, he had his identification card from where he worked at Webster Industries. Not being familiar with Webster Industries, I still wasn't sure what the crap bags were all about. However, I was happy to be able to finish issuing the citation and allow the man to be on his way.

A couple of days later I ran into Alan Rambo, a policeman in Rockford (one of the two-man force that was later reduced to one) who had worked at the Montgomery Police Department for twelve years previously. I began telling him my story. I explained how I couldn't understand where the man worked and when I asked him what he did he had told me, "Make plastic bag put crap in." Immediately Alan told me the man worked at Webster Industries. I was amazed how quickly he deciphered the situation and asked how he knew that. "They make colostomy bags" was his reply. Man, what a difference a little bit of information can make.

The next month, the defendant's adult daughter accompanied him to court and served as an interpreter. She stated the man wanted to plead not guilty since he did not understand me when I had asked if he had any other weapons. I was sworn in and gave the details of the encounter. The judge said he could see how there could be a communication problem; however, that did not change the fact the man was in violation of several laws and regulations and he should pay his fine and costs and consider himself fortunate I did not write him several tickets. The daughter explained to the man what the judge had said and he dejectedly left the courtroom.

I ran across a lot of people with different professions in my career; however, to the best of my knowledge that was the only crap bag maker I ever arrested. You can't make this stuff up!

"OMG!"

WHILE THE ENFORCEMENT of game and fish laws and regulations was our primary responsibility, we regularly ran across violations of other laws. As Alabama Police Officers Standards and Training–certified officers, we could enforce any law or regulation in Alabama. While some folks might think that sounds good, enforcing laws other than our own was often an aggravating undertaking. This was true in part because we often were not intimately familiar with some of the laws and it often tied us up at the time and later in court. Of course, there were occasions when you needed to take some action.

One spring morning I was headed toward Sylacauga, the nearest town to the Coosa Wildlife Management Area, to pick up some needed supplies when I came up behind a vehicle driving very erratically. Anybody can cross the centerline and a single incident normally doesn't cause me much angst. However, when a driver repeatedly crosses the centerline on an already narrow two-lane road, it catches my attention. As I followed the small car, it was obvious the driver was distracted. This was before everyone had a cell phone and texting while driving was a huge problem as it is today. I decided I needed to stop the vehicle and see what was going on.

"OMG!"

I activated my blue lights and the car eventually pulled to the side of the road. As unusual as it was for us to make a traffic stop, I'm sure it was more unusual for a driver to look up and see they were being stopped by the game warden! I approached the vehicle and observed a young woman behind the wheel and a young child in the backseat. I identified myself and asked to see the woman's driver's license. I told her I had observed her crossing the centerline several times and asked if she was having a problem. It was obvious she was not happy about being stopped. I wasn't sure if that was because I was a game warden or if it was her general attitude toward law enforcement. In an accusatory tone, she said she did not realize she had crossed the centerline. I told her I would be back with her shortly. I noted she did not appear to be disoriented or under the influence of anything.

I returned to my truck and contacted the sheriff's office dispatcher and had her check the status of the driver's license. She quickly called back and informed me the driver's license was expired. I checked the date and found the license had been expired for several months. While most enforcement officers would allow up to a month of a grace period on expired licenses, several months was too long. I decided to issue her a ticket for the expired license and a warning for failure to maintain her lane. I returned to the vehicle and asked her to sign the ticket. Although she was very unhappy, she signed the ticket and was on her way.

The next month I was in the district court. Unfortunately, game and fish cases and other misdemeanors were always set for nine o'clock and traffic cases were not heard until all other cases were adjudicated. That often made for a long day. I had searched the court docket and found the woman's name was on it, which meant she had not paid her ticket off beforehand. However, it was not at all uncommon for folks to come in and pay the ticket on the day of court. When this occurred, the case did not always get removed from the docket prior to court so we had to wait until the defendant's name was called.

I scanned the courtroom and eventually spotted the woman who I thought was the one who had received the ticket. I must admit I have been fooled before. Although it may have only been a month since I encountered the defendant, let me assure you people's appearance can drastically change from the time you encounter them on the road or in the field to the time they appear in court. I have had folks who had a heavy beard in the field but appeared in court clean-shaven. Some who on the road had long hair and shabby clothes but appeared in court clean-cut and in a suit. Believe me when I tell you folks can change their appearance to the point they are hard to recognize. In the cases where the defendant doesn't show up for court until three or four months later, it can be really difficult.

As was his general practice, after the judge had finished with the misdemeanor docket he took a short recess. In a few minutes he returned ready to take up the traffic docket. The folks on the traffic docket sometimes took it tough depending on how the earlier cases had gone. If there had been several preliminary hearings or a testy trial, the judge might not be in a good mood by the time the traffic cases were called. When that was the case, it was usually folks' best bet to plead guilty and get things over with. However, there were always a few who knew the trooper had hit the wrong car with his radar or they had come to a complete stop at the stop sign and they didn't know why the officer said they hadn't. Some folks just had to roll the dice.

Fortunately, the judge seemed to be in a pretty good state of mind and started going through the docket. The defendants would form a line in front of the judge's bench and the officers would stand off to the right side until they were needed. One of the things that was sure to happen in traffic court was the driver who would claim they were not going as fast as the speed that was listed on the ticket. I observed this literally hundreds of times. The judge called the case and the defendant would step forward. The judge would say you've been charged with driving seventy-four miles per hour in a fifty-five mile per hour zone, how do you plead? They would plead not guilty. He would ask why they pled not guilty and the defendant would reply that they weren't going that fast. The judge would ask how fast they were going and they would say seventy. The judge would then say "The court finds you guilty on your admission of speeding" and would advise them they needed to go and pay the clerk. This would happen several times each court date. It happened so much that it got to be humorous.

In among the speeding tickets, the judge called the name of the woman who I had written the citation for the expired license. The young woman approached the bench. She was probably about five feet and two inches tall and maybe one hundred pounds. The judge looked down from the bench and asked how she pled and she replied, "Not guilty." I must admit I found it interesting that someone would plead not guilty to driving with an expired driver's license. To me, the expiration date on the license was pretty plain.

Seeing that I was the one who had written the ticket and knowing that was uncommon, the judge suspected there was more to the case than the license being expired. He called me to the bench and instructed each of us to raise our hand and be sworn to tell the truth. He asked me why I had written the lady a ticket. I told him I had come up behind the vehicle on County Road 41 and observed as the driver had crossed the centerline multiple times. I had stopped the car and she had denied crossing the centerline. I ran her license and found out it was expired and I issued her a citation for that offense and a warning for failure to maintain her lane.

The judge looked at the woman and asked her if she had any questions she wanted to ask me. She said she did not. He asked why she had pled not guilty. She replied she didn't think I could write her a ticket for an expired license when that was not what I had pulled her over for. The judge asked why she thought I would have said she was crossing the centerline. This was when it got interesting. Although she had denied to me that she had crossed the line, she told the judge she could have possibly crossed the line because she was turned around in the seat feeding her child in the backseat some Vienna sausages for breakfast. The judge immediately blurted out, "Oh my God!" I thought the judge was really taking exception to her taking her eyes off the road while driving with a child in the car. However, I learned that wasn't the only thing he was upset about when he exclaimed, "You don't feed a kid Vienna sausages for breakfast!" While I didn't think that really had much to do with a driver's license being expired, the judge said, "The court finds you guilty. You need to go and pay the clerk." He looked at me and simply shook his head in disgust.

You can't make this stuff up.

BIRD PSYCHE
(DIDN'T SEE THAT COMING)

IN MANY DIFFERENT STORIES I have claimed the ringer on my home phone was attached to my seat at the table. It seemed every time my rear end hit the seat, the phone rang. It is impossible to know how many calls I fielded during my career but suffice it to say it was a lot.

One evening, as I was sitting down, I received a call from a woman who, once she had verified who I was, said she had a question for me. She explained she had rescued a baby bird from a Burger King drive-thru. She said she had taken the bird to a veterinarian who told her it was a baby dove. However, she soon learned it was a starling.

While the woman's tone gave me no reason to think she wasn't legitimate, I was skeptical and thought it might be a prank call. I was doing my best to recognize the voice but was having no luck.

Something I have tried to emphasize to many young officers is the necessity to be able to anticipate. It is extremely important. When you work in an arena where every encounter has the potential of turning deadly, you need to try to stay a step ahead. In the field, it is imperative that you listen intently and anticipate what is coming next. Anticipating a suspect's defense or lie helps you to counter it and hopefully get to the truth of the matter. Even in something as benign as a phone call, it is still wise to anticipate what question will be next.

The woman explained she had grown very attached to the bird. She said it sometimes sat on her shoulder as she worked in the kitchen. However, lately the bird had begun to fly into the windows and into her sliding glass door. She said this was making her think the bird was wanting to go outside. I thought that sounded pretty normal for a bird.

There was a brief pause and I anticipated the woman was likely struggling with the difficult decision as to whether or not to release the wild bird that had become her pet. Mustering her courage, the woman moved forward and asked me if I thought she should have the bird's wings clipped? Now I was the one remaining silent. I must admit that was not the question I had anticipated. Before I could answer, the lady moved on to her next question. She asked what I thought it would do to the bird's psyche if she had its wings clipped? Once again it took me a few seconds to come up with my answer. I told the lady I was not a bird psychiatrist, but I felt that birds were made to fly and therefore I believed the wing clipping procedure would be detrimental to the bird's psyche. She thanked me and hung up.

I never heard any more from the lady and no one came forward admitting to it being a prank. Therefore, I assume it was on the up-and-up. That was far from the only call I received from folks who had taken a wild animal and tried to domesticate it. The list of animals was long, with the favorites being raccoons and deer. Early on we issued permits for people to keep wild animals; however, luckily that practice ended and it became illegal to possess them. That definitely didn't stop folks from keeping them but it did make it more expensive!

Talk about not seeing something coming. I sure had not anticipated my conversation with the woman ending the way it did. However, isn't that how much of life happens? Sometimes you don't see it coming. The Lord says we had better keep our eyes open because he will return in the night like a thief without warning. You have received your warning. Jesus is coming back to claim that which is his. You can sail on wings like eagles or you can have your wings clipped. The choice is yours.

INVISIBLE FENCE

WHILE MOST PEOPLE IN ALABAMA would probably say they enjoy seeing deer, that is only true as long as they aren't wearing a deer as a hood ornament. Deer-vehicle collisions are frequent in Alabama. It rarely failed during hunter education courses as I explained the state owned all wildlife that someone would ask, "Why doesn't the state pay for their deer hitting my car?" Believe me I knew their pain.

Obviously when you have something causing as much damage as deer-vehicle collisions, you always have someone looking for some way to solve it. To that end, deer whistles were a common sight on the front bumpers of cars in the south. The idea was the "whistles" would emit a tone that would keep deer from running into the road. Research has shown numerous times the whistles are not effective. However, they are still sold regularly and a lot of folks swear by them.

Around the year 2000 or so a new product came on the market for homeowners. The invisible fence was a system where the landowner buried a "fence" around the perimeter of their yard. A collar was placed on the family pet. When the pet would get too close to the fence, it would receive a shock which would keep it in the yard. Although I never tried one, I understand they worked fairly well with some dogs.

I had a wildlife biologist friend in Utah who shared her invisible fence experience with me. She had three goats she was trying to keep contained to a lot behind her home. She installed the fence and put the collars on the goats. She explained it worked initially but soon the goats were once again on the prowl in the neighborhood. She replaced the batteries in the collars and the beasts were again contained. After going through this scenario a few times, she began doing some investigation. Her surveillance revealed the goats would stand close enough to the fence to activate the collar but not receive the full shock. They would withstand this tingle until they ran the battery down and would then go where they pleased!

An elderly woman who attended church with me called me one evening stating she had heard of an invention that might really help to reduce our high number of deer-car collisions. She explained how the invisible fence worked. Knowing the woman to be a serious type, I did not think she was pulling my leg. I was searching my mind on how to explain to her the problem with her idea when she asked, "What do you think?" I told her that while it sounded good in theory, the difficult part would be catching all the deer and putting the collars on them. She replied, "Well it's just a suggestion." I thanked her and we hung up.

Others thought it would be a good idea to put the "fence" around their shrubs and flowers that were being devastated by deer. Again, I would have to explain to them that while it sounded good in theory, it was very difficult getting the deer to wear the required collars! I kid you not. You can't make this stuff up.

HOW BIG AN OLE BOY ARE YOU?

IF YOU READ MY FIRST BOOK, *Parables from Poachers,* you may recall the first seventeen years of my career I was an area biologist on the Coosa Wildlife Management Area (WMA). In that position you wore many hats. I should say many, many hats. Managing a thirty-eight-thousand-acre wildlife management area encompassed many duties. There really wasn't much slack time.

Fall was a very busy time. Not only was I trying to plant fifty or sixty wildlife openings on the WMA, I was working with as many as eighty deer management clubs across twelve counties. Sandwiched in between those duties, I was always keeping an eye out for any violations that might crop up. Rarely did I have time to dedicate to strictly law enforcement.

One late fall afternoon as I was going about my duties, I had stopped by the WMA check station. The check station was a very small metal building measuring eight feet by ten feet. It contained a wooden desk, a file cabinet, and a couple of chairs. On days of a gun deer hunt it might also contain five or six people. To say it was too small was a gross understatement. As I was getting in my truck to head home, I heard a gunshot. I immediately placed the shot on Coosa County Road 29 just south of my location. County 29 formed the eastern boundary of the WMA for several miles. I quickly headed toward where I thought the shot came from and sure enough saw a truck sitting on the side of the road with a big guy with a rifle in hand standing beside the door. As I passed the truck the fellow slid into the driver's seat. I spun around in the road and came up behind the vehicle.

Working enforcement while not in uniform carried with it some problems. Folks who did not know me often did not realize I was a law enforcement officer since I might be wearing blue jeans and a work shirt. That was how I was dressed this day. I exited my truck and approached the driver. I introduced myself as the manager of the Coosa WMA and asked what he was up to. I could see he had the "Oh no, I'm caught" look on his face. I asked if he had a firearm and, after a brief hesitation, he said he did. I told him to hand it to me and he handed me a .22-caliber rifle. I asked if he had any other firearms and he said he did not. I carried the rifle to my vehicle and then returned to the man.

I advised him of his rights and asked him what he had shot at and he unconvincingly said he had not shot at anything. At that point, I gave him "the look." The look is a disgusted facial expression that tells the violator you do not believe what they are saying and are disgusted they are even trying to lie to you. It often works wonders. After giving him "the look," I employed "the implication." The implication is a tremendous tool for the law enforcement officer. It is often a great way to solicit an inference from subjects. In this case, I simply said, "Man, I was just right up there," as I pointed up the county road. The implication was I was just up the road and was watching when the fellow had shot. I didn't say that, but that was the inference I hoped the man would draw from what I had said. The truth was I did not know what he had shot at, but I did know he was the only person in the vicinity. He again said he had not shot and I quickly asked, "Then what were you doing?" He hesitated, obviously trying to quickly formulate a good lie. He replied, "I heard some dogs running and thought they might run a deer across the road." That was better than I could have hoped for. He had just confessed to hunting from a public road, possibly hunting from the aid of a vehicle and hunting without a permit. Believe me when I tell you it normally wasn't that easy. I did not let on that he had just confessed. Instead, I quickly asked, "You heard dogs running while you were driving down the road?" He said he had. I said, "So you pulled over here to try to get a shot if they ran a deer out? "Yes," was his reply. What else could he say at that point?

I asked to see his driver's license and told him to sit tight. His license revealed his name was Myron Dawson and he was from Sylacauga, which was about fifteen miles up the road. I went back to my truck and began digging out my ticket book. Although I did not need to know what the fellow had shot at for the charges to be valid, I was wondering if he had actually shot a deer. While I had seen a few deer killed with a .22 rifle, it wasn't the typical deer gun. I was contemplating whether to try and get more information or to just go with what I had seen and what he had said.

I wrote the man a ticket for hunting from the public road and returned to his truck. As I explained the bond to the man, something interesting happened. The WMA was located forty-five miles north of Montgomery. Montgomery is home to Maxwell-Gunter Air Force Base and was also the home of the Alabama Air National Guard. This close proximity meant we frequently had C-130s, F-16s, and small trainer jets flying over, often at treetop level. The jets would often appear out of nowhere with a deafening roar that would definitely get one's attention.

As fate would have it, a jet screamed overhead and movement in the bed of the man's truck caught my eye. I stepped back and looked in the bed of the truck. There were several items in the truck; however, I quickly located the source of the movement. It was the wing of a large red-tailed hawk. The loud noise had evidently startled the bird. Obviously, there should not have been a hawk in the bed of the truck. Closer examination revealed the bird had been shot. I asked the man how the bird had ended up in his truck. Interestingly, the once cooperative subject now decided he did not want to answer any more questions. I told him that was fine seeing how some things spoke for themselves. I completed another citation and told the man I would see him at court.

A couple of days later, I received a phone call from a fellow who identified himself as Jerry Barber. He explained he was a federal probation officer and asked if I had encountered Mr. Dawson a couple of days earlier. I said I had. He asked if I could give him the details of the incident. I explained how I had come upon Mr. Dawson on the side of the road and he had claimed he had heard some dogs running and was stopped there hoping to get a shot at a deer. He asked if Mr. Dawson had possessed a firearm and I told him he had. He said that was all he needed to know and it would likely be enough to send Mr. Dawson back to prison for a year. He asked if I would be able to give him a written statement and I said I would. He hesitated and then asked me a question I definitely had not anticipated. He said, "How big are you?" I told him I was five feet eleven inches tall and weighed about 275 pounds. He said the reason he asked was he had received several complaints concerning Mr. Dawson in the past; however, no one had ever been willing to press any charges against the man. It seemed he was a pretty rough fellow and most people were scared of him. I told him he was a big man but he had not given me any problem. He said he appreciated my cooperation and would be back in touch if necessary.

I could not help but get tickled at the probation officer's question. A few years before this incident, there was a radio DJ who played a fictional character who did comedy sketches and phone pranks. Although the stories changed it usually went that the guy would be talking smack over the phone and would eventually get to the point to where he was going to meet the person on the line and put a whipping on them. However, before he would end the conversation and head their way he would ask, "How big of an ole boy are ya?"

Mr. Dawson was a big boy and I'm thankful he didn't want to give me any trouble. It was always interesting when folks tried to formulate a story on the spur of the moment. Some of them were good at it and some were not. One of the things I did not understand was why this guy was still standing outside of the truck with a rifle when he had obviously already retrieved the hawk and put it in his truck. Of course, it could have been he had shot the hawk earlier and was now standing outside the truck hoping a deer would come running by. Either way the man pled guilty to his charges in district court and was then escorted back to prison for a year!

DEPUTY DAN
(I'VE GOT 'EM)

THE RINGING OF THE PHONE woke me from a deep sleep. As I reached for the receiver, a quick glance at the clock showed it was 2:35 in the morning. A call at that time of the night was pretty common during the deer season in Coosa County in central Alabama. Before you think I'm complaining, let me assure you I'm not. As a matter of fact, one of my pet peeves throughout my career as a wildlife biologist and conservation enforcement officer was people who would NOT call and report night hunting when it occurred. They would often call the next day and tell me about it or worse yet would tell me after the entire season was over. A few times, I received a complaint from a landowner concerning shots the night before and I would have to tell the complainant I was within a mile or two of their location and sometimes I had to tell them I had heard the shot but was unable to pinpoint it. Had they called my home, the jail, or my cell phone, I could have in all likelihood apprehended the violators.

I always told landowners or anyone else who knew something was going on to contact me when it happened, not the next day or week. I hoped the now-ringing phone meant there was something in progress. I answered the phone and the county sheriff's office dispatcher told me unit 105 had some night hunters stopped and needed assistance. She advised he was at the Willingham's on County Road 40. The Willingham place was like a lot of places in the south. No one had lived there for years. However, that was the way it had always been known. Today, there is no evidence anybody ever lived there; however, it is still how the place is known. I told the dispatcher I would be en route shortly and hit the floor running.

Coosa County Sheriff's Deputy Dan Bearden's call sign was 105. To me Deputy Dan was bigger than life. He was a consummate professional. Having been in law enforcement for many years, he taught me a lot about enforcing the law while I rode with him on patrol. Dan was probably five feet eight inches tall and weighed in at about 290 pounds. However, if you ever shook his monstrous hand or spent any time around him you would swear he was eight feet tall! Dan had a presence that emanated confidence, power, and authority. Many times I witnessed him stopping or preventing an altercation simply by arriving on the scene. The respect he enjoyed had been earned. Dan was shown respect by many people who weren't the type that normally would do so. However, many of them knew for a fact Dan Bearden could straighten out a U-turn if he thought it needed doing.

There is a dangerous fallacy out there today. The media and many politicians want everyone to believe there should not be any violence associated with law enforcement work. I do not know where the idea originated that officers should be able to subdue and arrest violators without any use of force or even raising their voice. I've often thought it would be a good idea to require a mandatory ride-along for district attorneys, judges, politicians, and activists so they could receive a firsthand view of what law enforcement officers face on a daily basis. I believe the majority of officers do a masterful job of measuring their response to the situations they are placed in. Dan once told me the details of an incident where he had been dispatched to a domestic violence call where thirteen people were fighting on the front porch of a house in a small south Alabama town. He said there was no backup available so he proceeded to the location to see what he could do. On arrival he found an interesting melee taking place with both men and women involved. Let's stop there so you can evaluate the situation and decide what you would do. There are thirteen people engaged in a brawl. There is no backup available. I'll give you another split second to decide on your response. I know the odds don't sound good but you need to remember that law enforcement officers face similar situations on a somewhat regular basis. When his loud verbal commands fell on deaf ears, he said he waded into the fray and began separating people on the porch. After tossing five or six out into the yard, someone jumped on his back and stuck a sharp object into his throat. In an effort to get them off his back, he swung his baton back over his shoulder and ended up splitting the assailant's head open. Although totally outnumbered and under assault, he was charged with police brutality. Although he was cleared, that type of situation is what keeps a lot of folks from entering the profession today.

 I knew Dan wouldn't be calling me at two in the morning unless he had something worthwhile. Once in the truck I headed toward his location, which fortunately was only about four miles from my home. I radioed him and told him I was en route. He informed me he was holding three night hunters for me and I told him I appreciated that. I hoped these were the outlaws who had been the cause of several recent complaints of shots fired between 2:00 and 4:00 a.m.

 For me, complaints between two and four in the morning were the worst. I had grown accustomed to working until one or two in the morning. I had no problem getting up and leaving the house around three or four. However, I had a very difficult time staying out all night. I guess that was when burning the candle at both ends caught up with me. I could stay out there all night, but I was not very effective. Even though I had developed the skill of being able to hear a shot and even carry on a conversation in my sleep, which I did on many occasions, that normally wasn't happening between three and four.

I will tell you it was a lot easier to get up and going when someone was holding the culprits for you. However, I can count on one hand the number of times that happened. I heard Dan call "1741," as that was my radio number at the time. I answered and he said he had just heard a high-powered rifle shot. I asked where he thought it was and he said he would place it very near Mrs. Dunlap's house. As fate would have it I was passing directly in front of Mrs. Dunlap's house. I keyed the radio microphone and said, "I'm at her house now." Just as soon as I unkeyed the microphone, I topped a rise in the road and there I observed a small pickup sitting crossways in the highway with an individual standing beside it holding a high-powered rifle. I again keyed the mic and exclaimed, "I got 'em!" I switched on my blue lights and soon the local paperboy and his accomplice were in custody.

I called Dan and told him to bring his three on to the jail and we would sort them all out when we got there. He soon arrived and we proceeded with the volumes of paperwork it took to write up five individuals for fifteen charges! Amazingly, I did not receive another complaint between two and three in the morning that season!

Dan was always good to help us, as were the vast majority of deputies I had the pleasure of working with. Dan was a true mentor to me. He was very wise concerning how the criminal element thought and acted. He could see an individual standing around and basically tell you what was on his mind. He knew who was dealing what, how, and where. He could read people better than any officer I ever worked with. That went for officers as well as violators. I hate to have to admit I have known some officers I wouldn't trust to tell me it was raining. Unfortunately, when you work in law enforcement you often become quite cynical and untrusting of others. You learn to make a judgment about others within a few seconds of meeting them. Although you are sometimes wrong, you are normally pretty much correct. This is good in that it may save your life; it is discouraging in that you often get a feeling about someone that you know is probably right but you wish it wasn't. Dan was an excellent judge of character and I don't know of anyone I would have rather had on my side.

At the age of about sixteen, Dan's daughter, who suffered from spina bifida, died. Although he knew this day would come, it was devastating for him. Soon thereafter his marriage fell apart as well. The stress was tremendous and it soon caught up with the mountain of a man. One April morning, Dan began experiencing chest pains in the courthouse. The sheriff rushed him to the hospital, where he died a short time later of a massive heart attack. I think a piece of me also died that day. Dan's was the first law enforcement funeral I had ever attended. The cars were lined up for as far as the eye could see. The funeral home was packed with fellow officers. Everybody knew Dan. His death hit me hard. However, I was better able to accept it knowing I will one day see him again in heaven. What about you? Will you be reunited with those who have gone on before? That depends on the decisions made by both parties. Choose wisely. See you soon, Dan.

TRAINED GATOR

ONE SPECIES OF WILDLIFE I had very little contact with during my career was the alligator. Fortunately, central Alabama had relatively few alligators. I say this is fortunate since those areas of the state that had many alligators ran departmental personnel ragged trying to capture and relocate the pesky reptiles. Since for much of my career the alligators were totally protected, the public was not allowed to solve alligator problems on their own. Even in the latter years when the state initiated an alligator season, albeit limited, alligators were still protected. Therefore, whenever a gator was spotted in a farm pond or lake, we would get a call.

Conservation Enforcement Officer Earl Brown once received a call from a landowner who was very upset and stated we had to come and remove an alligator from his pond. Since I was a freshly minted wildlife biologist, he felt it would be good for me to accompany him on the nuisance wildlife call. We traveled to the southeast part of the county and met with the lake owner. It was obvious from the start the man was upset. He told us in no uncertain terms the removal of this dangerous animal had to be our highest priority.

While many folks we dealt with wanted something done "right now" that often wasn't how it worked. It wasn't that we didn't want to assist this fellow; however, removing an alligator from a pond on the back forty didn't seem to us to be the emergency this guy was making it out to be.

We took a cursory look at the pond and explained to the man we would come back and monitor the pond and figure out the best way to remove the creature. It was obvious our lack of a sense of urgency didn't sit well with the guy. He forcefully told us we didn't need to wait and watch anything. As we let his statement uncomfortably hang in the air, he followed up by saying he could show us where the alligator would come out on the bank and eat chicken. I immediately didn't like the sound of that and asked him just what he meant. Getting more frustrated, the man said, if we would put chicken on the pond bank, the alligator would come out of the pond and eat it.

While this fellow was aggravated, as we say in the south, he was "fixin'" to see someone who was aggravated. I think my tone may have given away my anger when I growled, "How do you know that?" He was not so quick with his response so I again demanded to know how he knew this fact about the gator. Realizing he had already stepped in it and there was nowhere to go now, he admitted he had put chicken out for the gator to eat. I countered with, "So you have trained this alligator to come out on the bank and eat?" His attitude was a little less condescending when he lowered his head and offered a dejected, "Yes."

Neither Earl nor I said anything for probably a minute. The man hung his head. His tone was much more conciliatory when he stated he realized he had made a bad mistake. He went on to tell us he had a two-year-old grandchild that loved to come to the pond, but now he was afraid to bring the child to the area with the alligator coming out on the bank. While it wasn't very professional, my anger got the better of me and I commented that was why he shouldn't have trained it to do that.

After letting him think about it for a bit, we told him we would clean up his mess. A gator trained to come and eat on command turned out not to be very difficult to wrangle.

I think we would all do well to realize that some of our problems are of our own making. Today, the concept of taking responsibility for your own actions seems very foreign to many folks. We will all reap what we sow. The sooner we understand that, the better off we will likely be.

DEFICIENT SAMPLE

Working as an area wildlife biologist my enforcement activities were sometimes slow during the summer months. That was a good thing seeing how I had plenty of work trying to keep up with the demands of a 38,000-acre wildlife management area and technical guidance activities for landowners in twelve counties. However, early on I realized it was easy to get rusty during the off season as far as keeping a sharp enforcement eye goes. Therefore, I would often work with the officers checking fishing and with the county deputies, city police, and state troopers. This led to many adventures.

My favorite deputy to work with was Dan Bearden. Dan was bigger than life. Although he only stood about five feet eight inches tall, after you got to know him and watched him work you would swear he was a giant. He commanded respect and there was no back up in him. Dan would run into situations others would run from. If he was scared of anything, I never knew it.

The town of Kellyton, in northeast Coosa County, was Dan's primary domain. He lived there and policed there and everyone knew him. The area had many mobile home communities and was a perpetual source of calls for assistance. Dan had his finger on the pulse of Kellyton. These days you often hear the phrase *community policing*. I can tell you it makes a tremendous difference when the officer knows the people he is policing. When working with Dan you would swear he knew everyone and what the majority of them had done or were thinking about doing.

We were conducting some surveillance one night when we observed a vehicle driving in a very erratic manner. It looked just like the NASCAR drivers when they are going from side to side, cleaning their tires off before a restart. The driver would go from one side of the county road to the other. It was so exaggerated I felt certain it was someone who knew we were there and was trying to pull one over on us. However, when the car passed us we did not recognize it. Dan pulled out behind the car and activated his blue lights. The car soon pulled over and we approached. The driver was a guy about forty years old and drunk as Cooter Brown. (I don't know who Cooter Brown was but I've heard that saying all my life.) We got him out of the car and helped him to our vehicle. There are few sobriety tests a suspect can perform when they can't stand up. We placed him under arrest, secured his vehicle, and headed to the county jail.

The man was not unlike most drunks I have dealt with in that he would change from happy to sad to mad to happy at the drop of a hat. We got to the jail and helped the man in. He literally could not walk under his own power. We sat him down in a chair, started the paperwork, and turned on the Intoxilyzer.

The Intoxilyzer was the machine that determined the alcohol content of a driver's blood. After the machine warmed up, I escorted the man to the machine. Dan explained the test and handed the man the tube he would have to blow in. The man blew in the tube but only in short bursts. I do not believe he was at himself enough to try to beat the test but after several attempts he failed to provide a sufficient sample. When this occurred the subject was charged as refusing the test. In this case we received what was called a deficient sample. This meant the machine had detected blood alcohol content (BAC) but had not gotten enough to be considered a complete sample. Although the reading would not be usable in court seeing how it was officially a refusal, it did give some insight into the person's level of intoxication. At the time the legal limit was .10 BAC. I felt certain this guy had to be over the limit; however, without a proper amount of breath to test I feared the deficient sample might be below the limit. Even though I thought he was extremely intoxicated, I was not prepared when I looked at the deficient sample print out and it was .32!

We escorted the man back to the booking room and sat him in a chair. I watched as he repeatedly tried to place a quarter on a small ledge and each time it would fall off he would laugh hysterically. We had begun the process of getting him booked in and soon came to the part where I told the man I would need to take his belt. The man had been happy and easy going until this point. When I said I needed his belt he jumped up and assumed a fighting stance and said, "I have to ask my wife for my belt." I was amazed the fellow was able to stand up on his own. I told him I would have to have the belt and he said I couldn't. I wasn't sure just how to proceed so I looked at Dan with a "what do I do now" look. He placed his finger to his lips motioning me to be quiet. I walked back over to the booking desk and the man sat back down.

We finished the paperwork and Dan told the man he needed him to stand up. He stood up and Dan told him to put his hands on the wall. He began frisking the man. As he patted him down, he unhooked his belt and slid it out. He handed it to me and I placed it in the bag with his other belongings. The man never missed the belt as Dan placed him in a cell.

About a year later I heard the subject had died. It seems after a night of drinking he had driven home. However, he was so intoxicated he passed out before making it into his house and died due to exposure. I saw many people who allowed alcohol to ruin their lives and many lives of those around them. Every time we arrested someone for DUI, I could not help but believe we had likely saved their life and the lives of others. Don't drink and drive. As a matter of fact, just don't start drinking in the first place!

YELLOW MARSHMALLOW PEOPLE

I NORMALLY ALWAYS ENJOYED working with Conservation Enforcement Officer (CEO) Jerry Fincher. My association with Jerry was an interesting one. I met Jerry when he accepted a teaching job at the middle school where my wife taught. My wife, Melanie, was his teaching mentor. He began calling her his "mother figure." If you are old enough to remember or if you have watched *The Andy Griffith Show* on TV Land you have likely seen an episode which featured Ernest T. Bass. Ernest T. was a rock-throwing country hick. In one episode, Ernest T. had decided he needed to get an education. He was far from a regular student. The local teacher did try to teach him. Her efforts reminded him of his mother and therefore she became his "mother figure." It was an interesting year for Melanie. Not only was she mentoring Jerry, she also was the mentor for an Alabama college football standout who after a brief professional career became a schoolteacher. Let's just say, it was a year to remember.

The first time I met Jerry, he told me his true goal was to become an Alabama game warden. To that end, he had already served a couple of internships and was currently on the game warden register, meaning his application had been accepted and he was waiting for us to get the green light to hire some folks.

The next year he was hired as the CEO for Talladega County and I guess you could say I became his "father figure." He actually referred to me as his field training officer (FTO). We did not have an official FTO program at that time. I took him under my wing. He was a good student and today is the lieutenant for the district.

One fine fall day I was riding with Jerry in Talladega County when we received a call from the district office stating a woman, Mrs. Barclay, had called and requested an officer to come to her residence. Jerry looked at me and rolled his eyes. The caller went on to tell Jerry the captain had advised he did not need to go on the call by himself. That comment definitely got my attention. Seeing how we all answer numerous calls a year, normally alone and without any close backup, I wasn't sure what to make of the captain's comment. I looked at Jerry with the look that asked, What the heck is that about? He explained Mrs. Barclay had some significant mental issues. He said she regularly saw "people" who weren't really there and those "people" were killing hundreds of deer on her property. I thought to myself this was going to be interesting. I was oh so right!

When we arrived, Mrs. Barclay was standing in her driveway. Jerry pulled in and stopped with Mrs. Barclay outside of his window. Immediately, I could tell this was indeed going to be interesting. She was standing facing her house with her right shoulder toward our truck. When Jerry cheerfully asked, "How are you doing today?" she looked at us out of the corner of her eye and did not say anything for probably twenty seconds. While she was still not looking toward us, she stated she was having the same problem she had had previously with the aliens killing deer. Jerry asked her if she had seen any lately and she motioned with her head toward the road and said, "There's one in that bush out there right now." She added, "I can see his eyes." At this point, she turned one hundred and eighty degrees so she was facing the road. She told us there was "another one" across the road under a trailer lying on a pillow. Hard as I tried, I didn't see anything.

Jerry asked her if she had seen anyone near the house, which was what she had complained about previously. Pointing at a pine tree near her house, she said "Blue Shirt" had been in that tree earlier. She explained he always wore a blue shirt so she called him Blue Shirt. She said he had killed a whole pile of deer but had taken them away before we arrived. Jerry glanced at me and I could tell by the look on his face that the look on my face was probably pretty humorous.

The lady was now staring right at us when she said she was sick and tired of "them" shining their lights into her house. She said although she had covered her windows with aluminum foil, "they" would shine their lights on the ground and it would reflect up into her house. After she said that, she took off toward her house at a fast pace. Over her shoulder she said she needed to show us something. I was beginning to understand why the captain had not wanted Jerry to come here by himself. I looked at Jerry and asked what he thought she might be wanting to show us and he said there was literally no telling.

Within a minute she was coming back toward us with a plastic Walmart bag in her hand. As she approached Jerry's window she said, "These are some of the masks they wear." I again thought to myself, This is going to be interesting. I was not disappointed. She reached in the bag and with a knowing look, she pulled out one of the "masks." It was a sheet of sandpaper! How do you respond to that? I knew Jerry was thinking the same thing because his delayed response was, "Wow!" We were not finished. She said the masks were what emitted the light they reflected into her house. While I was a bit baffled on how that worked, I was very much baffled by this whole situation.

I guess by this point I shouldn't have been surprised by anything; however, I was. I just thought I had a slack jaw up until this point. The woman placed the sandpaper back in the bag and said, "I've caught a bunch of little yellow marshmallow people and I have them in a cardboard box in my house. Do you want to come and see them?" While I was thinking that really would be something to see, Jerry quickly told her we really couldn't stay. She shrugged her shoulders and headed back toward her house carrying her bag full of "masks."

Just as she reached the steps, the front door opened and a man stepped out. Mrs. Barclay went into the house and the man came walking out to our truck. As the man neared our location, Jerry told me he was Mr. Barclay. The man sidled up to the truck and asked how we were doing. Jerry told him we were fine and were answering the complaint about the hunting. He asked the man if he had seen any deer that had been killed. He laughed a little and said he had not seen any. Jerry asked if he had seen anyone in the trees around the house. He again giggled and said he had not.

This was a difficult situation to interpret. I wasn't sure how to read it but I had the feeling this guy was in a bad situation. His answers to our questions seemed to indicate he understood what his wife had been reporting really wasn't taking place. I was thinking it had to be pretty difficult to live in such a situation and was surely not something he wanted to be discussing with two game wardens he did not know. Jerry pressed forward and asked the man if he had ever seen any of the aliens in the yard or across the road. The man again said he had not seen any of that. This was a situation where you don't know whether to say you're sorry about his situation or just drop it and get out of Dodge. Just as I was about to suggest to Jerry that we get on our way, the man said, "Now, I *have* seen some of the little yellow marshmallow people."

As I was staring at the man with my mouth hanging open, Jerry was thinking fast on his feet and said, "They aren't killing any deer, are they?" The man said they were not and Jerry told him we were going to have to get to the next call. We backed out of the driveway and headed down the road. I looked at Jerry and said I didn't believe that had really happened. Shaking his head, Jerry said he needed to call the office and tell them we were off the call. The captain answered the phone. Jerry told him we had just left the residence and he had a question for him. He asked, "Do you know anything that can be done with a box full of little yellow marshmallow people?" The captain did not miss a beat and replied, "It sounds like you need to build a fire and start sharpening some sticks!" We all busted out laughing. Jerry gave the captain the gist of what took place. The captain commented, "It takes all kinds."

Jerry had to deal with these calls for years. This situation helped me to understand that fielding the calls concerning sightings of black panthers and little honey bears really weren't that bad at all. I realized that even my meeting with the woman who claimed people were nefariously cutting the twigs off the trees around her yard was actually a walk in the park. But that's another story.

Y'ALL'S SNEAKY

REGULARLY DURING MY CAREER, I would work with the county deputies. I sometimes rode with them on routine patrol and I eventually became a reserve deputy. I worked with them as an investigator on active cases and worked on the cold case task force. Solving cold cases brings a great feeling of accomplishment. I also enjoyed working traffic with them. I found it a great way to sharpen my skills.

One night I happened to be at the jail and agreed to accompany a young deputy to a domestic disturbance call in the east part of the county. While my job as a conservation enforcement officer was a dangerous one, I would much rather go to a night hunting call than one for domestic violence.

It seemed a live-in boyfriend had been moved to the porch and it appeared he did not appreciate it and took out his frustration on the woman's car. He had left the scene before we arrived and we were taking a report and making some photos of the damage. As we gathered information from the female resident, her mother, and her aunt, the mother came around to where I was and seeing the wildlife and freshwater fisheries patches on my shirt asked, "Are you a game warden?" After I told her I was, she cocked her head to one side and said, "Y'all's sneaky." I laughed and asked

Y'ALL'S SNEAKY

why she would say such a thing. She said she had been fishing under the bridge on Highway 63 when she heard something in the woods behind her. She looked around, but not seeing anything, she resumed her fishing. She said the next thing she knew, there was a game warden standing right beside her asking to see her fishing license. She said she almost jumped in the creek and then added "and you know I didn't have no license."

Now let me tell you this certainly wasn't the first thing I had been accused of during my career and I had been called much worse! As a member of the game and fish department we were often the target of many accusers. One interesting instance comes to mind. When the coyote numbers really began to increase, we were accused of releasing coyotes in the state. The myth was we had introduced coyotes into the state at the request of paper companies who were upset because deer were eating their pine trees. The theory was the coyotes would eat the deer that were eating the trees. While it's true that deer eat some pine trees and it's true that coyotes eat some deer, trying to control the deer population with coyotes is not a winning strategy. If you introduced coyotes to cure a deer problem then you would end up with a deer problem and a coyote problem!

I had heard this myth many times; however, one of my supervisors, Ken, enlightened me on one aspect of the introduction process I had never heard before. He said he had a fellow in his county who confronted him about our introducing the coyotes. Ken said the irate resident was positive we had done this and there was no convincing him otherwise. The complainant told him a good friend of his had actually seen us releasing the coyotes. It was usually always someone else that was the actual witness. The man explained "his friend" had seen us dropping the coyotes from a helicopter. Hearing that, Ken told the man he wasn't sure a coyote would survive being dropped from a helicopter. The man was obviously one step ahead of him and told him we were dropping them from the helicopter into a farm pond! I would say you can't make that stuff up, but evidently someone did!

I told the woman that we had been accused of being sneaky from time to time. She told me when she had appeared in court the judge told her if she would go buy a license he would dismiss her case. She told me she went right then and bought a license, before he could change his mind.

With some of what went on, being accused of being sneaky wasn't a bad thing. As a matter of fact, I sort of resembled that remark!

TRAFFIC COURT
(THE CAR I WAS PASSING)

I FEEL CERTAIN every law enforcement officer could probably write a book based on the excuses they have been given. While I have heard my share of excuses working with game and fish, I tended to hear more denials. However, when working with the Coosa County Sheriff's Office I did hear some interesting excuses. It was interesting to me when someone stopped for speeding would offer the excuse that they were not familiar with the road. I always wanted to reply that I normally drive as fast as possible when I don't know the road. Another common response from speeders was the driver was almost out of gas. I guess everyone knows the faster you drive the more gas you save. Of course, everyone has heard of the driver who was trying to get to a restroom or the hospital or home before their curfew.

I believe a major problem that affects most drivers is the belief that our driving is always perfect. I've heard this put in a very understandable way. Everyone driving slower than me is an idiot and everyone going faster is a maniac. Now tell the truth, have you never thought that? I thought so.

Early in my career our district court judge would handle all other cases before calling the traffic docket. He would have the defendants form a line and would hear their cases one by one.

Unfortunately for them the judge had already been on the bench for a few hours and was normally pretty testy at that point. To say he wasn't in the mood for any lame excuses was an understatement.

One of the most interesting things that occurred in the traffic segment of court was the large number of folks charged with speeding who would appear and plead not guilty. When the judge would ask why they pled not guilty they would respond they weren't going that fast. The judge would use the same procedure for every one of these cases. He would say, "You were charged with going seventy-eight in a fifty-five-mile-per-hour zone." They would respond, "I wasn't going that fast." He would ask, "How fast were you going?" and they would say, "Seventy," and he would say, "The court finds you guilty on your admission of speeding, next case." This occurred time after time after time. Of course, every once in a while, there would be an alternative explanation.

While working with Coosa County Sheriff's Deputy Shane House, we stopped a car traveling eighty-three miles per hour in a sixty-five-mile-per-hour speed zone. The driver was issued a citation. She appeared in district court the next month. When the judge called the case, she stepped forward as we did. He informed the woman she had been cited for speeding and asked how she pled. She replied, "Not guilty." The judge instructed all of us to raise our hands and be sworn. He asked the deputy to tell him why he had written the ticket. He advised we had met the vehicle that appeared to be traveling at a high rate of speed. He activated his radar and it showed the car was going eighty-three miles per hour. We stopped the car and issued the driver a ticket.

The judge looked at the defendant and asked if she had any questions for the officer. She said she did not. He asked her why she felt she was not guilty. She told the judge the only reason we stopped her was because we had seen the out-of-state tag on her vehicle. The judge looked at Shane and asked him if that was the case. He replied, "No your honor." He quickly added that it's very difficult to see the tag on the rear of a vehicle at midnight when you are meeting them on the opposite side of the mediated four-lane highway. With a very disgusted look, the judge asked the driver if she had anything else to say. She did not. She was found guilty!

While working traffic enforcement on Highway 280 in Coosa County an Alabama State Trooper met a vehicle traveling at a high rate of speed. His radar indicated the driver was running eighty-six miles per hour in a sixty-five-mile-per-hour zone. He stopped the vehicle. Upon stating the reason for the stop, the driver informed the officer he felt he had not clocked him but had recorded the speed of the car he was passing. The driver continued to tell the officer how he had made a mistake. The trooper told the driver he was going to issue him a citation for speeding but the driver was welcome to come to court and plead his case before the judge, who was always interested in knowing how well or how poorly the officers were performing in the field. Not happy, the driver took the ticket and gruffly told the officer he would see him in court.

Two months later the driver appeared in court where he pled not guilty to the charge. When asked by the judge why he was pleading not guilty, the driver repeated the same story to the judge informing him the trooper had not clocked his car but had in fact clocked the car he was passing. The judge looked at the fellow and asked him to repeat his answer. He repeated his defense. The judge then asked him if the car he was passing was going eighty-six miles per hour, how fast did he think he was going? At this point, the driver finally realized what he had been saying all along. He told the judge he thought he had misspoken.

The judge told him he had heard enough and found the man guilty and issued the maximum fine.

As I said earlier, every once in a while, a case would come along that was definitely deviant from the norm. The judge called out the name on the ticket and a young man stepped up to the bench. The judge studied the ticket for a minute and then said, "It says here you were driving down the road with your butt stuck out the window. How do you plead?" You never knew what was coming next!

The problem these people had was they were all guilty. It is difficult to come up with a suitable excuse when you are guilty. That surely doesn't mean people don't try. They remind me a lot of us. Yes, me and you. We are guilty but we still keep looking for that excuse to get us out of it. Here's a hint: in the end, there isn't one! All have sinned and come short of the glory of God. Every knee will bow and every tongue will confess Jesus is Lord.

HUNTER HARASSMENT
(I TOLD YOU SO)

As I have written several times, for the first seventeen years of my career I worked every weekend of the long Alabama deer season. There were a couple of years where Christmas fell on a Saturday and we were off but that was rare. We worked so much during the deer season we had little time to hunt and frankly when you worked it each day, the hunting lost some of its luster. However, I learned to compensate for this during the turkey season. I did my best to hunt most days of turkey season. Of course, work and other obligations would sometimes get in the way, but I limited that as much as possible.

A few years back during the spring turkey season we received a complaint from a landowner about a fellow who had been known to stray across a property line. He said the man was hunting without a permit on some property next to his and felt certain he would be hunting on his property as soon as he heard a turkey gobble. He obviously wanted something done about the situation.

Knowing the fellow's previous exploits, as well as his high potential to violate the law, I checked things out and learned he did in fact possess a permit for the property he was hunting. The neighboring landowner was informed of this; however, he felt certain the man was only using the property as a jumping-off point to hunt his land. The fellow had reason to believe such seeing how it was a very common practice. However, as I have told many complainants, thinking and knowing are two different things!

Many wildlife outlaws were very adept at obtaining permission to hunt on property adjacent to larger, well-managed properties where they wanted to poach. Having a permit for the adjacent property allowed them to claim they had mistakenly crossed the line if caught. Many would overtly park their vehicle on the permitted property. Therefore, if we were to check them at their vehicle, as we often did, they would be on the proper property. Of course, if we suspected them of crossing the property line, we would work the line. Oftentimes a permit to hunt a forty-acre parcel would allow the outlaw the ability to access three or four adjacent properties comprising hundreds of acres. It was an effective technique and difficult to police.

The next week we received a call from the fellow hunting the neighboring property stating the adjacent (complaining) landowner was harassing him every time he tried to hunt the property. This prompted another visit to the original complainant. He was informed, once again, the fellow could legally hunt the property he was on. Furthermore, he was told he would be in violation of the law if he was harassing the man when he tried to hunt. His response was, "You know he is hunting on me." He was told if the man was in fact on his property he could sign a warrant on him; otherwise, he needed to leave the man alone or he would be the one in trouble.

A week later on a beautiful Saturday morning I had been sparring with an old gobbler and as usual he had got the best of the exchange. I arrived home and as I entered the door the phone rang. It was the sheriff's office dispatcher and he asked if I could come to the office and meet a complainant. That really wasn't what I wanted to do on a Saturday morning but I told him I would be en route. I made the short trip to the jail and there found the landowner who had originally complained about the fellow hunting on him. He was obviously highly agitated and immediately began explaining he had been shot at by the guy hunting adjacent to his property and he wanted the man arrested.

I asked him to start at the beginning and tell me what had happened. He said he had been on his property that morning and had observed the fellow on the adjacent property. He had mounted his four-wheeler and proceeded to drive up and down the property line and on his second or third pass the man had shot at him. I asked why he was driving up and down the property line and he became frustrated and told me I knew that guy was trying to hunt on his property. I reminded him he had been told not to continue harassing the man and that was exactly what he had been doing by riding his four-wheeler up and down the property line. I told him we would look into it. He became more irate and said he guessed it was okay for the man to shoot at him and stormed out of the office.

I phoned the fellow who had allegedly done the shooting and asked if he would come to the sheriff's office and speak with me. He soon arrived. I asked if he would go through the events of the morning for me. He stated he had gone to the property where he had a permit to hunt. He was walking across the property when the adjacent landowner came riding by on his four-wheeler. He stated the man had ridden by three or four times, revving the engine in an obvious effort to disturb him and disrupt his hunt. He said when the man came by again he fired his shotgun into the air and the man took off. I asked him if he had shot at the fellow. He gave me a look that was part aggravation and part whimsical and he replied, "You know, if I shot at him, he'd be shot!" I simply nodded my head. He asked, "Isn't it illegal for him to harass me like that?" I told him it was. He said he would like to press charges and I advised him to go to the clerk's office on Monday and the circuit clerk would allow him to sign a warrant for hunter harassment.

The Alabama interference with persons legally hunting or fishing law states:

> No person shall willfully and knowingly prevent, obstruct, impede, disturb, or interfere with, or attempt to prevent, obstruct, impede, disturb, or interfere with any person in legally hunting or fishing pursuant to the rules and regulations of the Department of Conservation and Natural Resources and the law of the State of Alabama.

With the landowner clearly in violation, the clerk issued the warrant and the landowner was arrested.

The next month found all three of us in district court. The judge called the case and we all approached the bench. The judge asked why the warrant had been signed on the man and the complainant explained what had occurred. The judge asked the defendant if he had in fact been riding up and down the property line on his four-wheeler harassing the man. The defendant began trying to explain to the judge he was trying to keep the man from hunting on his property. The judge asked him if the man was on his property or the adjacent property when this had occurred. The man said he was on the adjacent property but—that's when the judge cut him off and pronounced him guilty as charged.

This was the first hunter harassment case I ever dealt with. Seeing how the harassment law was put in place in response to anti-hunters disrupting hunts across the country, I never thought about it being used in the way it was in this case; however, to the best of my knowledge this is the predominant way it has been utilized in our state.

It was unfortunate this situation occurred, especially after the defendant was told point-blank what would happen if the harassment continued. Some folks don't believe stuff stinks until they step in it. I understand the aggravation that comes when someone feels their property is being violated; however, once again there is often a lot of difference between thinking and knowing!

GOT ANY PRIOR ARRESTS?

"JOEL, WHERE ARE YOU?" I knew by the tone in his voice my good friend Andy Hughes, the biologist aide on the Coosa Wildlife Management Area (WMA), had something going on. I responded I was at the sheriff's office. He excitedly told me he had found some people in an unauthorized area on the WMA and he thought they might be the thieves we were looking for! I told him I was on my way.

As an area biologist for the Alabama Department of Conservation and Natural Resources Wildlife Section for nearly eighteen years I can assure you a good biologist aide or assistant was a tremendous asset. The duties on a WMA are numerous. The Coosa WMA was thirty-eight thousand acres in size and provided hunting opportunities for small game, big game, and waterfowl. It had as many as three campgrounds, a shooting range, and two hundred miles of roads open to the public. Simply keeping encroaching limbs cut back along the roads took several days, not to mention cleaning out culverts and grading the roads. The campgrounds were in constant need of attention. In addition, we normally planted sixty acres of wildlife openings, trapped mourning doves, monitored hog traps, painted miles of boundary lines, and posted thousands of signs. Andy Hughes did all of this and more on the Coosa WMA. To say he was my right hand would be a gross understatement.

After I left the WMA to become the private lands biologist for central Alabama, Andy assumed an even larger role on the WMA. Now he was calling me for assistance and I knew I would do whatever I could to provide it.

Earlier that morning Andy had discovered a burglary had occurred on the WMA and the thieves had taken some oil and had siphoned the gas from some vehicles. Now he had found some tracks he thought might be a match on a closed road. Although Andy was the president of the Coosa County Sheriffs Reserve Unit, he had no law enforcement authority on the WMA and his supervisor was on vacation.

CCSO Sgt. Eddie Burke accompanied me as I made a quick trip to the WMA and found Andy waiting with the road blocked. We drove past the No Vehicles beyond This Point signs and the metal gate that had been torn down. At the end of the road on a sandbar on Weogufka Creek we found two vehicles and four people. There were two tents set up on the sandbar with a small fire burning. I may not have mentioned this was in the summer. If you haven't had the opportunity to enjoy a summer in Alabama, you should. Everyone in Alabama spends the summer near the water. I do not mean they go to the beach or the creek or a swimming pool; I mean the water is right there in the air all around us! The humidity is tough and why on earth anyone would want to have a fire going at 1:30 in the afternoon was beyond me, not to mention there was a WMA regulation against it.

I approached the two men and two women who were lounging in the water. One of the women immediately asked, "Are we doing something wrong?" I identified myself and told her we would discuss everything in a minute. I asked if anyone possessed any weapons. As they were all exiting the water, one of the men stated he had a machete in his tent. I asked if they had any weapons or anything illegal in their vehicles. They collectively said they didn't think so. I realize some folks are nervous during any contact with law enforcement and they may not put much thought into their responses to our questions; however, "I don't think so" is much different than "No."

I asked if they knew they were on the Coosa WMA and they stated they did not. This was a little difficult to believe seeing how they had driven past probably a hundred WMA signs on their way to where they were. I told them they were on the WMA and many regulations applied, one of which was there was no camping allowed except in designated camping areas and this wasn't one of them. I explained how all vehicles on the WMA were subject to being searched and we were going to do that while they began to disassemble their camp.

Eddie began searching the car while I searched the truck. Almost immediately I located a meth pipe. I called Eddie over and pointed it out and he retrieved it. We finished searching the vehicles and gathered the folks and informed them of all the regulations they had violated. They had driven down a road closed to traffic and onto a sandbar closed to traffic. They possessed alcohol, which was a violation. They were camping in a restricted area. They had a fire, which was illegal, and they had cut down a few small trees, which was also a violation. They were looking pretty pitiful by the time I finished the list. I conferred with Andy and Eddie and decided to write the two vehicle owners a couple of tickets each and arrest the guy for the drug pipe.

Writing a ticket under the blaring sun in one-hundred-degree weather isn't the easiest thing to accomplish for a fat boy. I had to retrieve a towel from my truck and continually wipe my arm to keep the sweat from soaking the ticket book. I still could not comprehend why on earth this group had a fire going and was tempted to write them for that as well! I finally finished the tickets and explained the bonds. The folks hurriedly loaded all of their equipment into the truck and I had the truck owner follow me to the jail. While that was a little unorthodox, I had learned way back that our department and others frowned on us loading folks in the bed of our truck and taking them to jail! It was not necessary for everyone to go to jail; however, since the owner of the drug paraphernalia was also the owner of the truck with all of their belongings in it, they all decided to go.

At the jail, we went into the supervisor's office and Eddie began the case paperwork. Since the man who claimed ownership of the meth pipe had an ID card and not a driver's license, I assumed his license was either suspended or revoked. When I asked what he had been arrested for in the past he hesitated and then said he hadn't been. I wanted to say I was born at night but it wasn't last night, but instead I just gave him my disgusted "I know you're lying" look. He was slow to respond but finally explained he had been in a building with some guys who had some meth in a shaker bottle and he had got arrested but since it wasn't his, the charges were dropped. I asked if that was his only previous violation and he indicated it was. When I asked if his driver's license was suspended or revoked he replied, "Oh they're suspended, they suspended them before I got out of prison." I almost laughed out loud, but I kept my composure and asked what he had been in prison for and he said, "Marijuana first." As it turned out, the fellow had actually been in court three months earlier for a meth possession charge and somehow (even with a prior felony drug arrest) had been placed on probation. I could not believe it when we contacted the county where he had been placed on probation and they did not revoke him. It was very evident our system was broken. (And it's much worse now!)

HE'S STILL SHOOTING

It was interesting how according to him his only previous arrest had been a misunderstanding about a meth lab in which the charges were dropped and yet he had been to prison and was currently on probation! I wasn't sure which part of previous arrests he didn't understand but evidently it was all of it!

Three weeks later the defendants appeared in district court. The judge called the cases and the two defendants and I approached the bench. I was surprised when the first defendant pled not guilty to operating a vehicle in an area not open to traffic. I raised my hand and swore to tell the truth and explained to the judge the folks had driven down the road where the gate had been torn down and onto the sandbar at Shoemaker Cave past a multitude of bright yellow signs indicating special rules and regulations applied. The judge asked the defendant why he pled not guilty and the man replied they didn't tear the gate down and there were no signs along the road as I had said. The defendant did not know I had a card up my sleeve so to speak, but he was about to find out. The judge reviewed the ticket, gave the man a hard look, and said, "There were plenty of signs and the gate was up when I was there three weeks ago!" It was interesting watching the man melt right there in front of the bench. The ace up my sleeve was that our district judge rode his dirt bike on the WMA on a regular basis. The defendant's untruthful defense did not sway the judge, who quickly found him guilty.

After seeing his cohort dismantled by the judge in front of everyone in the courtroom, the second defendant pled guilty to his WMA violation and to possession of drug paraphernalia. He was assessed fines and court costs totaling over $500. He was given a month to pay his fine and court costs and if everything wasn't paid in full, he would be required to serve sixty days in jail. I must admit I was not shocked when the next month a warrant was issued for his arrest for failure to pay. Then again, based on what he had told me, he may have just been confused as to whether or not he had been arrested! You can't make this stuff up!

CAREFUL WHAT YOU ASK FOR

RETIRED COOSA COUNTY SHERIFF Terry Wilson and his wife, Ran, are good friends of mine. After distinguished careers in the US Air Force, they moved to Coosa County. Terry became a deputy and moved up until he was elected sheriff. He faithfully served in that office until he decided to try a real retirement.

One of the things he initiated in our county was a neighborhood watch program in the various communities across the county. The monthly meetings were a great opportunity for the sheriff's office to share with and listen to the folks in the county. As with most things in the south, some good eating was usually associated with each meeting.

Although the deputies who handled the meetings would often have an agenda to go by, they never really knew what might come up. During one such meeting after the deputy had concluded his program he received an earful from the folks in attendance. It seems the members of the watch group were some more upset about people speeding up and down the rural county road in front of the fire department/meeting hall. The deputy in attendance took the complaint to heart and contacted the trooper post and requested additional patrol for the area.

A couple of days later, early in the morning our local trooper had visited the area and found the complaints to be warranted.

He issued eight speeding citations. You would think that the group would have been elated; however, that was not the case. Every ticket went to a neighborhood watch member!

I understand at the next meeting the talk revolved around how to get the speed limit on the road raised!

That incident reminded me of another similar situation. After the new centralized school was built for the county, local residents along County Road 49, which ran behind the school, were worried about the school kids who were "flying" up and down the road. My friend, Trooper Brad East, was dispatched to curtail the illegal activity. It didn't take long until he had his first violator. It wasn't hard to spot seeing how it was a big yellow school bus! The next vehicle to come "flying" down the road was an older resident who lived on the road. As the trooper began writing the ticket, the man protested, saying, "I'm the one that called and asked y'all to come over here." The trooper replied, "We're here!"

I have written several "That's not what we wanted" stories. Things often do not turn out how we want. I could write you a long list. However, when we study it we often find out things turn out the way they do based on what we do. While that is definitely not always true, many times it is. Even when we do our best, we fall short. All have sinned and fallen short of the glory of God. However, the gift of God is eternal life through Jesus Christ our Lord. It can't be bought. It can't be earned. It must be accepted. If you want to ask someone for something, ask Jesus for forgiveness. Do it today, while the opportunity still exists. Praise the Lord for His saving grace.

CAN'T CATCH THEM ALL

AT THE HEIGHT of the four-wheeler craze the Coosa Wildlife Management Area (WMA) seemed to be ground zero. With two hundred miles of roads open to traffic there was no shortage of room to roam. Unfortunately, it seemed the roads didn't possess the same allure as the power line right-of-ways and road banks since that was where everyone wanted to ride. This was a violation of a WMA regulation prohibiting the operation of motor-driven vehicles in areas other than roads open to regular four-wheel traffic. Although folks rode the area day and night every month of the year, summer was especially busy. It wasn't unusual to check fifty or more riders in a few hours.

One Saturday about dusky dark I was set up on the underwater bridge road, which was the main road that traversed the WMA. I was stopping every car, truck, and ATV that came through, looking for anything illegal but primarily firearms. After a brief lull, I heard the telltale sound of multiple ATVs coming my way. I had set up just around a curve in the road, which gave me a little of an element of surprise. When the riders rounded the curve, I activated my blue lights and stepped into the road with my flashlight in hand. The two men brought their four-wheelers to a stop directly in front of me. Although the weather was hot I thought the men were sweating pretty good to have been riding along in the open air. In addition to being sweaty the pair also appeared to be pretty nervous. Although it is very common for people to be nervous when they encounter law enforcement, after a while you learn to determine whether it's just "normal" nervous or "hinky, I'm guilty of something" nervous.

The WMA was somewhat unique in that Alabama state law stated anyone inside the boundaries of the WMA was subject to search without a warrant. This included any vehicle, hunting sack, coat, or pocket. We were allowed to search for anything that would be illegal to possess on the WMA. Seeing how this included a .22-caliber cartridge, the search authority was very broad.

Realizing these guys were sort of hinky and not seeing any reason why, I decided I should have them empty their pockets. This revealed nothing out of the ordinary. A thorough look at their ATVs also failed to turn up anything. Not finding anything, I allowed the men to go on their way and I soon called it a day and headed home with an uneasy feeling that I had missed something.

A couple of weeks later I was approached by an acquaintance who began to ask questions concerning my checking four-wheelers on the WMA. After a couple of minutes of general chitchat, he asked if I remembered checking a couple of fellows about dark and I told him I checked dozens of fellows around dark. Wondering where this was leading I told him I wasn't sure who he was talking about. He added I had made the pair empty their pockets. I told him I did remember that stop. He went on to say the guys had told him they were so nervous you couldn't have driven a pin up their rear end with a sledgehammer. I agreed they had been pretty nervous but I didn't know why. His reply of "I can tell you" got my attention. He said the pair was extra nervous because they were the first two of four ATVs and they had been sent out ahead to make sure the coast was clear before the last two, which were loaded down with freshly cut marijuana, came out. I wasn't sure what I was supposed to say to that so I just said, "Well, you can't catch them all." As often was the case, the guy couldn't wait to point out I had missed the load of marijuana; however, as was also common he was not willing to share the names of anyone involved.

I had just got home from a hard day on the WMA when the phone began to ring. For years I swore there was a button on my seat at the table that when I sat down it made the phone ring! It happened much too often for it to be a coincidence. The caller asked if I was Mr. Glover and I told him I was. He said he had something he needed to tell me but he did not want his name involved. I told him that probably wouldn't be a problem since I did not know who he was.

The man told me he had been on the WMA earlier that day and had found a patch of marijuana. I asked where it was and he gave me detailed directions and I didn't think I would have any problem finding the area. I asked how many plants were there and he said there might be fifty plants. I told him I appreciated the information and would look into it. He reminded me again he did not want his name mentioned and I advised him I still didn't know his name.

I called my local forester/officer, Blake Kelley, and asked if he wanted to accompany me on a marijuana hunt on the WMA and he said he would. I asked him to meet me at the WMA checking station the next day at around lunch and we would see if we could find it.

Blake showed up the next day and we headed to the area. The directions were good and we pulled right up to the patch, which was in an old log-landing area. You always had to be vigilant when dealing with a dope grow. There was always the possibility it might booby-trapped or even guarded by someone. We did not see any evidence of anyone around so we pulled out our machetes and began cutting the plants down and loading them on my truck. The patch was scattered over about a third to a half of an acre. I had told Blake to keep a count of each plant he loaded on the truck. When we finally finished collecting the plants we added our numbers and learned that maybe fifty plants had blossomed into 436!

We carried the plants back to the WMA check station and off-loaded them in the parking lot. I called Deputy Brett Oakes and asked him to come to the check station. Brett soon arrived and we soaked the plants with diesel fuel and set them on fire. You never caught them all, but sometimes you got more than what you anticipated. Working the thirty-eight-thousand-acre WMA, I am sure I missed a whole lot more than I ever caught. It wasn't something you could dwell on. You did the best you could with the time you had.

Realizing the relatively low number of people we apprehended makes me appreciate my good judges that much more. Of course, if you listened to many of the violators we did apprehend you would understand it was the first time they had ever violated the law! If I had believed I was that lucky, I should have bought a bunch of lottery tickets. I haven't bought one yet!

ORANGE HATS ON THE DASH

WHILE WE STAYED REALLY BUSY during the deer season checking baited stands, working hunting without a permit complaints, and the ever-present hunting deer at night calls, every once in a while, normally during the middle of the week, there was a slack day. In addition, there were many days during the deer season when we either did not have time to get to the next baited site or did not have some other violation to work at dark. On these days I would often look for a vehicle sitting on the side of the road or in the woods. Reasoning the vehicle belonged to a hunter, I would set up surveillance and wait on the owner to return. When the hunter would come out it would give me an opportunity to check their license, permit, and ammunition and verify they were wearing the required hunter orange. This tactic resulted in numerous arrests.

I do not know why but for some reason many hunters like to carry their orange cap on the dash of their vehicle rather than wear it. They very often would wear a camo cap while keeping the orange in the truck. Although today it would probably be considered some type of profiling, finding a vehicle parked on the edge of the woods with an orange cap on the dash usually gave me the feeling a ticket might be in the offing.

One cool evening during deer season I had slipped away for a rare evening deer hunt. Not seeing any deer, I left the woods a little early and on my drive home I passed a truck on the property adjacent to my hunting lease and noticed not one but two orange caps on the dash. With my house only five minutes away, I hurried home, put on my uniform and jumped in the state truck and headed back to the vehicle.

During this time, it was too dark to identify your target at 5:15 p.m. I returned to the subject's vehicle at approximately 5:30 p.m. I was a little surprised to find no one had returned to the truck. I parked nearby and found a good observation point near the hunter's vehicle. Although this was a good technique, you had to be very careful when employing it. It was not a good idea to startle a hunter who likely was carrying a loaded firearm. I knew the property these guys were on wasn't large and they should be back soon.

Finally, I began to hear the voices of the approaching hunters. I had already decided I would allow them to reach the vehicle before I made myself known. Just as the voices were becoming clearer, a shot rang out in the distance. I illuminated my watch and noted the time was 5:48 p.m., an hour after sunset and a full thirty minutes after what I would call dark.

I was soon able to make out a couple of images in the dark. When the men reached the truck and opened the doors, I turned on my flashlight and announced, "State game warden." I asked the pair to place their rifles in the vehicle and I noticed neither man was wearing any hunter orange. I approached and asked to see their hunting licenses. I checked the licenses and commented on the lack of hunter orange. Each man stated he had orange in the truck. I asked if they had heard the shot in the distance just before they reached the truck. They acknowledged they had. I asked, "Do you think the guy who fired that shot could have seen your orange in the truck?" After a brief silence, one man said, "That's a good point." I wrote each man a citation and they both shook my hand and thanked me. I loved it when a plan came together!

RUNNING WHEN YOU SHOULD HAVE STAYED

EARLY IN MY CAREER, working dove hunting usually meant making a lot of cases. At that time, the law for hunting by the aid of bait had no reference in it concerning the intent of the person hunting. Therefore, whether or not a hunter had knowledge of a field being baited was irrelevant. If you were caught on a baited field, you were arrested. This often resulted in twenty, thirty, and even fifty arrests on one field. This wasn't difficult when the hunters either had no knowledge of the field being baited or thought they had covered their illegal activity to the point we could not find it. We would work our way around the field collecting licenses and would then write citations. When the hunters did know the field was baited they would often wear their tennis shoes. When we entered one side of the field they exited the other. Opening day was always good for a chase—or maybe several.

Dove season was not unlike any other in that the more effort you put in, the more you would get out. The weeks prior to opening day were spent roaming suspect fields, sometimes at night, looking for bait. It wasn't unusual to have twenty or more fields to check in some counties. In addition to baited fields, we would find legal fields we would plan to check after the baited fields and we would normally always hear shooting on other fields we had not located ahead of time. Opening day was always busy.

Our conservation enforcement officer (CEO) in neighboring Chilton County related to me an opening day story with a twist. Several officers were checking dove hunters on opening day of dove season when they heard shooting on a nearby field. After finishing with the first field, they proceeded to the next. Following the sound of the shots, the officer deciphered the location of the field and realized he knew whom the field belonged to. The officer entered the field and as he scanned the shooters he recognized one of them as the landowner. Just then the man ran from the field. Knowing where the man lived, the officer ran back to his vehicle and quickly drove to the man's house. He waited beside the house and soon the heavily breathing man came out of the woods at a fast walk. When he was within a few feet of the door, the CEO stepped out and asked, "Where are you headed?" The man dropped his head and stood in silence. The officer asked, "Is that field baited?" "No," the man replied. "Then why are you running?" "I don't have any license," was his weak response. "Don't you own that field?" the officer asked. "Yeah," was the dejected response. The officer hesitated for a moment and asked the man if he was familiar with the regulation concerning submitting to the inspection of a CEO. He went on to explain the regulation states a hunter is required to allow a CEO to inspect a game vest, coat, firearm, and so on, and failure to do so was a violation. The officer wrote the man a ticket for failure to allow inspection. He finished the paperwork and gave the man the ticket and prepared to leave. "Are you not going to write me for the license?" the man asked anxiously. "Nope," he replied and then added, "You don't need a license to hunt on your own property." I know he appreciated hearing that!

You know we have probably all run from authority at one time or another. Of course, there is no getting away from the ultimate authority. What about you? Are you running from God? Running is futile. Just like in this story, stopping and allowing a thorough inspection of your life might be just what is needed. There is no getting away. Maybe you need to stop and ask the Lord to forgive you. He will. It makes all the difference.

HOT SPOT BIOLOGIST

SOME OUTDOOR MAGAZINES were notorious for taking a little bit of fact and embellishing it beyond recognition. For that reason, we were always skeptical and hesitant to grant an interview and/or give much information. Obviously, as a public agency we were often required to talk with these guys. Of course they always wanted to know some juicy tidbit they could pass along to the reading public. One of their favorite topics was which management area in the district would offer hunters the best chance to take a good buck.

My supervisor received just such a request. After reviewing the harvest records for each area, it was obvious my area, the Coosa Wildlife Management Area (WMA), was producing more older-age-class bucks than the other areas in the district. In addition, the last hunt of the season coincided with the peak of our rut and was always our best hunt. Unfortunately, this information was passed along to the writer and it soon appeared in print in the Hunting Hot Spot column. The writer as usual had flowered things up and ended the piece with the statement that the district biologist says anyone wanting to kill a good buck should make the last hunt on the Coosa WMA.

You never knew whether or not the article would entice any additional hunters to give the area a try. Unfortunately, the articles often made it sound like there was a good buck hiding behind every bush just waiting on someone to stroll up and shoot them. This was often all it took to get some folks to show up and give it a try. On the day of the hunt, the numbers were basically the same as usual; however, we did have three hunters who made a trip from Kentucky specifically to try our "hot spot."

The WMA checking station was the hub of activity on days of a hunt. Although the crowd ebbed and flowed there were normally some hunters around most of the day. This was especially true around 9:00 or 10:00 a.m. since that was around the time deer killed that morning started showing up to be checked. It was required that any deer taken on the WMA had to be brought to the check station so we could collect biological data. We would weigh the deer and remove a jawbone so we could estimate its age. This information was valuable for determining the condition of the herd, which helped us decide how many deer we should remove from the property each year.

As I said earlier, this was normally our best hunt of the year when some of our largest bucks were taken. Therefore, we had several hunters crowded around the check station in hopes of seeing a good buck brought in. Anticipating several deer coming in, our whole crew, including our district biologist, was on hand.

Everything was running smoothly until the three Kentucky hunters arrived and it was evident they were none too happy. Their first complaint was there weren't even any trees on what they described as "this godforsaken place." Although that was an exaggeration, I must admit there had been a lot of timber removed from the property. Of course, when you understood that a timber company owned the property for the purpose of growing and harvesting timber, you knew that was going to happen. The irate trio then grumbled about the condition of the muddy roads and how they could barely get around on the area. Once again there was some truth to that. When you combined logging equipment, rain, log trucks, and hundreds of hunters' vehicles on a dirt-and-gravel road it got muddy. Some of it got really muddy. It was not unusual for us to get frequent requests to come and pull a truck out of a ditch. Believe me when I tell you it was a full-time job trying to keep the roads passable during a wet deer season.

Lastly, the leader of the group stated they had not even seen a deer track much less a good buck. Of course, most of the other hunters present had also not seen a good buck for if they had they would not be standing around waiting to see one. While none of these complaints were unusual, these guys were quite upset that they had spent the money for out-of-state licenses and made the several-hour-long drive not to be able to get around or see any trees or deer.

I had heard this kind of complaints before and I could understand their angst. However, they were not finished with their rant. The lead whiner stated he wished he could get his hands on the blankety-blank hot spot biologist who had recommended this sorry place. It was then I noticed my supervisor as he slowly moved toward his vehicle. He slipped inside his car and quietly drove away.

I told the man I could understand his disappointment and was sorry he had not had a better experience. I also told him it was unfortunate but you couldn't always believe what you read in those magazines. I wasn't sure but I got the feeling they weren't planning on coming back. It may have been the way they left slinging gravel and everything!

While the plight of these fellows wasn't funny, the fact that "the hot spot biologist" had snuck off was hilarious. We got on the radio and called our supervisor and told him the trio had left the check station in search of "the hot spot biologist." We told him when we turned around and realized he wasn't there, we had given them his vehicle description and they were out looking for him. We added they were a little irate so he might want to be on the lookout for them. That message was met with silence. When I was able to regain my composure, I let him off the hook and told him they had actually headed back to Kentucky and it was safe to return. A few minutes later he came driving up. He exited his vehicle and came to the check station. The first thing he said was, "I will never give another interview to a reporter!" As far as I know he never did. He was a good supervisor. I'm glad he survived the incident!

HOPE YOU ENJOYED IT

As THE AREA BIOLOGIST for Coosa Wildlife Management Area (WMA) for seventeen years, I spent a lot of time performing law enforcement duties. Since all land in Alabama is posted by law, wildlife management areas were one of the few places available for use by the hunting and nonhunting public. Although supported by hunters from the sales of hunting and management area licenses and matching federal money, the fact we did not own the areas usually meant they were wide open to the general public. While making the areas available to folks to view nature, hike, pick berries, and the like was good for public relations, it produced many problems. Although many folks were not hunting on the area, there was a long list of rules and regulations that applied to anyone using the property.

When the area became a mecca for all-terrain vehicles (ATVs) and horse riders a multitude of problems came to the forefront. During the height of the four-wheeler craze, I once had eighty-nine contacts with four-wheelers in a three-hour period! The Coosa WMA had approximately two hundred miles of road that could be legally utilized by ATVs and horse riders. However, it seemed the majority would rather ride through the woods and on the power line right-of-ways that crossed the area. Other favorite illegal riding areas were roadside red clay banks, fire breaks, and logging roads, especially those with water bars installed. A water bar is a berm of dirt constructed across roads and firebreaks on steep terrain to slow water flow and help prevent erosion. Unfortunately, these were evidently fun to climb over with ATVs as well.

Although I really didn't mind people legally riding ATVs and horses, this did create a major problem during the hunting season. For the life of me I could not understand why someone would want to ride a horse through the woods or on the roads of the area on the day of a scheduled gun deer hunt when you might have as many as eight hundred to one thousand hunters in the woods and driving the roads; however, on many occasions I found myself trying to persuade a group of horse riders to go somewhere else when they showed up to ride on a hunt day. We normally only had nine days of gun hunts on the management area for the entire season. Unfortunately, they were normally on weekends, which was the busiest time for everything.

Four-wheelers were probably a larger source of complaint than horses simply because of volume and the noise they created. One ATV wasn't that bad, but after a hunter had a group of six or eight roar by, especially when he had been calling a previously gobbling turkey, they were pretty ticked off when they reached me with their complaint. Therefore, we did our best to enforce our "no off-road use" regulations. One regulation stated it was unlawful for any person except authorized personnel to operate any motor-driven vehicle behind, under, or around any locked gate, barricaded road, or sign that prohibits vehicular traffic. Another regulation stated it was unlawful for any unauthorized person at any time to operate a motor scooter, motorcycle, trail bike, or any motor-driven vehicle on any AREA except on regularly used roads open for public use by four-wheel vehicle traffic. Obviously, it was also illegal to operate these vehicles on the paved public roads that traversed the area.

I remember one hunt in particular when another officer and I had left the check station to go and patrol the area. We had gone maybe a mile when I spotted two ATV riders climbing up a water-barred logging road about one hundred yards off the main road in an area that had recently been clear cut and replanted in trees. The area obviously was not open to four-wheel traffic. I knew where the riders would emerge when they got up the hill and my partner and I were waiting there when they came over the rise. I approached one of the riders and instructed him to turn off his machine and let me see his driver's license. To this request he gruffly responded, "What's your problem?"

Let me take you on a little aside for a moment. Now I definitely can't speak for all law enforcement officers everywhere; however, I can tell you that for me, attitude and demeanor were very important. Do not misunderstand me; if I caught someone in a flagrant violation they would more than likely get a ticket. If it was a premeditated violation such as night hunting, they would normally get at least three tickets no matter how contrite they were. But in many cases where someone was technically in violation, but a warning would suffice, I often, not always, went with a warning. Now let me clarify that by saying when I went to work we did not have the option of writing warnings. Therefore, you either wrote a ticket or nothing and that often meant a ticket.

About ten years into my career, we were given the opportunity to issue warnings if the violator deserved one. This made attitude that much more relevant. I will never understand why so many people feel it is their right to verbally abuse anyone wearing a badge. I guess you could say it was a question of demeanor. Because sometimes "da meaner" they got, the more I would write! Running your mouth was a good way to part with some cash.

HOPE YOU ENJOYED IT

During my career I told many people, "I don't know that I ever had anyone talk their way out of a ticket, but I had a lot of them talk themselves into one!" This four-wheeler rider was no exception. I countered his question of "What's your problem?" with one of my own. Do you know you are on the wildlife management area? "Yeah," he angrily replied while digging through his wallet for his license. I pointed to a nearby bright yellow management area sign and asked if he had seen those signs. I once again received a contemptuous "Yeah." "Those signs state this is a WMA and special rules and regulations apply," I explained. I went on to advise him one of those regulations states you can only ride four-wheelers on roads open to regular four-wheel traffic and this—pointing to the trail he was on—isn't open to traffic. That little fact only received a huff from the disgruntled rider. I took his license and promptly began writing his citation. I returned with the ticket and explained it to him and showed him where to sign it. In a still-harsh tone, he asked, "I don't guess there's no such thing as a warning for this?" "No," was my simple reply. He begrudgingly signed the ticket. As I was removing his copy of the ticket from my book, he said, "The dealership I bought this thing from said this was a good place to ride!" Although I knew it wasn't the best or most professional reply, but having had to endure his hostile attitude, I could not help myself and as I handed him the ticket I said, "Well take this back and tell them how much you enjoyed it!"

We headed for our truck and if looks could kill we would have never made it. I figured my comment would probably provoke a call from Montgomery or the man would have something to say to the judge in court. However, he called the judge and paid his fine and costs prior to court. Maybe looking back on it he realized how belligerent he had been and felt bad about it. Yeah right!

STOLEN PURSE AT CEDAR CIRCLE

COOSA COUNTY ALABAMA is a small county relative to many others; however, when you had to go from one end to the other in a hurry, it didn't seem like it. Such was the case one fall night when I accompanied Coosa County Deputy Brett Oakes on a wild ride.

Although on rare occasions you may receive a call close to your current location, it seems most calls are at least halfway across the county. We were in the south-central part of the county near Rockford when we received a call stating someone had committed a strong-arm robbery at Cedar Circle and had taken a woman's purse.

Cedar Circle was best described as a redneck bar located adjacent to the Coosa River pretty much in the middle of nowhere on the western boundary of the county. The only access to the area was via Lay Dam Road, a desolate stretch of road with a plethora of potholes and a white-tailed deer infestation. Calls to the bar were commonplace and we often referred to the trip as "running the gauntlet" since it always entailed dodging holes, bucks, and does. This night was no exception as we drove as fast as we could without losing a wheel or gaining a hood ornament! During the entire ride Brett was lamenting about how stressful it was and how he hoped the perpetrator was still on the scene so we didn't make the trip for nothing.

Arriving on the scene we noticed there were few vehicles in the parking lot. I hated going to the club since it was often frequented by folks I had arrested for game law violations and for some unknown reason they weren't always glad to see me. The place was basically two rooms side by side. The right-side room contained a couple of pool tables and the left side where the entrance was had the bar. We walked in and observed a lone woman sitting at the bar with her back to us. The bartender looked at us and nodded toward the woman. Sitting on the bar in front of the woman was a purse.

We approached the woman and Brett asked if she had reported her purse being stolen. She replied she had. He asked if the purse on the bar belonged to her. She said yes; she then said she had reported someone had stolen her purse because there were some people bothering her and she knew we wouldn't come just because people were bothering her. About the time the second "bothering her" came out of her mouth, Brett grabbed her by the arm and literally snatched her off the barstool. I felt certain she had just sustained a whiplash; however, there was no time to assess her condition as she was now face down on the bar being handcuffed. Brett looked at me and barked "Grab that purse!" as he was dragging her to the car. He flung her in the backseat and slammed the door and we were on our way to the jail. It was a quiet ride. We arrived at the jail and Brett escorted the woman inside. He told the jailer to put her in a cell and he began the paperwork for a charge of filing a false report.

I have arrested a lot of people and have seen a lot of people taken into custody, but I don't remember any who had a knot jerked in their butt any quicker than the woman at Cedar Circle!

CATCH HIM BY MONDAY

RECEIVING GOOD INFORMATION from the public was key to making good cases. If you figure the odds, it's a wonder we ever caught anybody. Although Coosa County was small by some standards, containing only 652 square miles, that was a lot of ground for two officers to try to cover. Without having a heads-up on where to focus our efforts we could spend a lot of time on likely looking places that never paid off.

With good information being such a valuable commodity, you can imagine how excited I was when I received a call from a woman needing to give me some information about someone night hunting deer. The night hunting of deer was rampant in our rural county. As with many violations, it seemed it was happening all over. However, if I was set up in the southeast corner of the county, the complaint would come from the northwest. Sure, we sometimes were in the right place at the right time; however, when we could receive good info it really improved our odds of success.

It was very unusual for a woman to call with information, but when they did it was normally good. I listened with interest as the lady told me there was a man who was night hunting deer in the Richville area. Richville was a small community in the southwest corner of the county. Like all of the county it was sparsely populated with people and heavily populated with deer.

The woman described when the activity was occurring, what type vehicle the culprit was driving, and even the type of weapon being utilized. There were just too many details for this to be secondhand or hearsay information, which prompted me to ask her just how she knew all of this. After a brief pause she told me the man committing the violations was in fact her ex-husband. This filled in a few blanks and made me a little uneasy but I couldn't help but think of the adage about a woman scorned. I kept listening. The woman gave a few more details and answered a couple of questions I had. I told her I would share the info with the other officers in the county and we would see what we could do to apprehend the individual.

After another brief pause the woman told me there was one more thing. This really piqued my interest. My mind was racing. She had provided so much info I couldn't guess what else there might be. "What's that?" I asked. "I need him caught by Monday," was her reply. Now I was thinking about another adage about the other shoe dropping. "Why is that?" I asked. "Because we have a custody hearing on Monday and if he gets arrested before then I can use it against him in court." I tried not to let her hear the disappointment in my voice when I told her I appreciated the information and we would see what we could do.

I passed the info on to the two officers in the county and both of them responded in the same way. Each one said they weren't sure when they would have time to get down that way. With that I knew they felt the same way I did. We didn't catch him, but I'm sure it was some good information.

That story put me in mind of another that carried an interesting motivation. A highlight of my career was to serve as the Assistant Turkey Project Leader. In this position I worked alongside Supervising Wildlife Biologist Steven Barnett. Steve and I both loved turkey hunting and considered it an honor to be able work on the behalf of the monarch of the woods, the wild turkey. Working on the turkey project afforded us the opportunity to serve on the National Wild Turkey Federation (NWTF) Technical Committee. The technical committee was made up of wildlife biologists from departments across the country and the NWTF biologists. It was an honor and a privilege to serve with these fine folks.

Let me take this opportunity to also thank and commend the board members of the Alabama chapter of the NWTF. It is comprised of a fine group of men who have worked steadfastly for the wild turkey and those who chase them in Alabama. They put their resources to work for the benefit of all conservationists in Alabama. I know of no other group that supports Alabama wildlife and hunters to the extent they do. It was my good fortune to have the opportunity to work with them.

One of the benefits of serving on the NWTF Technical Committee was that Steve and I attended the NWTF national convention in Nashville each February. While returning from the convention each year we made it a point to stop and have breakfast at Cracker Barrel.

We had just been seated when a man approached our table and asked if we were game wardens. I can't tell you how many times I have been asked that question. Although I was a certified wildlife biologist and the regional private lands biologist for central Alabama and Steve was the supervising biologist over the wildlife district in south Alabama, we each had law enforcement authority. Our actual state personnel title was conservation enforcement officer supervisor and we both made a lot of cases. I was many things, including a game warden, and, therefore, I simply answered the man's question with, "Yes." However, since we were in Tennessee I felt it pertinent that I inform the fellow I was an Alabama game warden. The man said that was fine and asked if I would stop by his table on my way out.

After finishing our breakfast, Steve and I stopped by the man's table. He began telling us a man he called a local thug and an accomplice had killed forty-two deer during the past week. I must admit, I had never received a complaint involving that many deer being killed in a week. He explained the violator worked as a horse trainer and lived on the Rob McKenzie Farm off of Clear Creek Road. He said his counterpart lived in Ardmore, Alabama, and added they hunted in both states.

The man stated it was just wrong what they were doing and they needed to be stopped. I told him I agreed and I appreciated the information. I sensed this fellow wasn't quite finished and I was correct. He took a deep breath and said he hated the guy that was doing this. The way he said it, I couldn't tell if he hated what the guy was doing or if he actually hated the culprit. I quickly received clarification when the man informed us he was about to go on trial for attempted murder and the violator he was reporting was the victim. He quickly assured me the charges were false. He said he wanted me to know everything so I wouldn't think he was just saying this stuff out of spite.

This was getting pretty in depth. I did not comment and the man continued to provide even more info. It seems he had carried his car to the guy to have some body work done and paid him $3,000 up front. He said the man kept the car for nine months and instead of fixing it, he sold the seats out of it and some other parts. He said when he went to retrieve the car, he got in a fight with the man and got charged with attempted murder. I assured him I appreciated the information and would pass it on to the proper officers.

We received information from a lot of folks with a lot of different motivations. I came to understand that motivation was an important aspect of life. I witnessed folks doing a lot of things with pure motives and just as many with not-so-pure motives. I learned to examine even my own motivation for what I did.

I always tried to teach new officers that anytime someone provided them with some information, they needed to try and decipher the informant's motivation. While most of the time the informant was simply opposed to illegal behavior, at other times there was much more in play. Many people will not hesitate to attempt to use law enforcement to get back at someone. If you don't believe that, you should attend district court and you will see it play out right in front of you.

These stories really do demonstrate a fact of life. Many people are users and manipulators. They work hard to have things benefit them and aren't afraid to use other people to get their desired results. Unfortunately, I'm afraid everyone may fall into that trap at times. The Bible says if our goal seems right to us, our motivation seems justified. However, we are often motivated by self-centeredness. The way we view things is often due to our sinful nature. We would do well to remember what the Bible says in Proverbs. All the ways of a man are pure in his own eyes, but the Lord weighs the spirit. God is the one who examines our heart. He knows our true motivation, no matter what we may say or convince ourselves of. We all have motivations and we all face temptations. This being the truth, we would all do well to call upon the Lord for wisdom. He promised if we ask for it, He will give it. The woman in this story had a deadline. Each of us has one as well. Unfortunately, we don't know when that day will come. That's all the more reason to get things right today. The Savior is waiting.

JUDGES

DURING MY CAREER, I was very fortunate to work with some judges who understood the seriousness of the violation of wildlife laws. This was made extremely clear one day in Coosa County District Court. I had brought a case for hunting without a permit to court. In Alabama, all land is posted by law. Anyone other than the landowner or the immediate family must have written permission in their possession to hunt on private property. It is the hunter's responsibility to know where they are. We made many arrests for hunting without a permit especially during the deer season.

This case was a simple one and the judge promptly found the defendant guilty and levied a fine of $500 plus applicable court costs. The next case on the docket was a domestic violence case. I listened to the testimony of how the male subject had attacked the female with a stick of wood and, in her assessment, had tried to kill her, although there were no severe injuries. A serious case nonetheless. After the judge had heard all of the facts, and there were interesting facts on each side, he was ready to announce the verdict and sentence. Although the male was somewhat provoked, he was guilty of an assault and the domestic violence rules were pretty clear. Therefore, I was not surprised when the judge pronounced him guilty. However, I'm sure that the illegal hunter who had just been fined was a bit shocked when the domestic attacker was given a fine of $25!!!!!!!

Attack someone with a stick = $25

Hunt without a permit = $500

Conservation-minded judge = Priceless

As I stated I was blessed to work with conservation-minded judges; however, this wasn't always the case. Some of these situations were aggravating, others disgusting, and some outright unbelievable. The very worst judge I had ever had the misfortune to bring a case before was the district court judge in the north end of Talladega County. This guy was some more piece of work.

On a cold winter night, I was working with Conservation Enforcement Officer (CEO) Jerry Fincher attempting to catch some folks night hunting for deer in the south part of Talladega County. We had just settled in for what might be a long vigil when the radio crackled to life with the voice of Jerry's partner CEO Greg Gilliland. Greg was still a novice as a game warden and had just started working by himself. Hearing the tension in his voice we knew we needed to head toward his location. Greg explained he had just apprehended five night hunters and needed some assistance. We advised we were on the way but it would be a while.

Talladega County is a large county geographically encompassing 760 square miles and is home to over eighty thousand residents. The county was ceded by the Creek Indians in 1832. *Talladega* means "border town" in the Creek language. It was the border between the lands of the Creek, Cherokee, and Chickasaw tribes. Today the county has five cities and around twenty towns and communities. The county is bordered on the west by the Coosa River and contains a large segment of the Talladega National Forest and a portion of the Hollins Wildlife

Management Area. White-tailed deer and wild turkey are plentiful, as is small game, and fishing opportunities abound throughout the county.

Like in every county, it was difficult to decide which area to work with night hunting of deer being prevalent everywhere. This night Jerry and I were along the county line in the southwest corner of the county near the Fayetteville community and Greg was near the city of Lincoln in the far northeast part of the county. The road distance between us was nearly fifty miles and to compound things a dense fog was rolling in.

We were traveling as fast as we safely could and yet we felt like we were crawling. We kept in radio contact as we strained to even see the roadway. Finally, almost an hour after receiving his call for assistance, we arrived at his location.

It was an interesting scene. There was one guy lying in the road handcuffed and four others sitting in the road beside him. We asked Greg to tell us what happened and he explained he had observed the driver of the vehicle manipulate his SUV in a manner to allow his headlights to illuminate a field on the side of the road. The driver had then backed up and continued down the road in the direction he was previously going.

This was a common technique used by folks hunting deer at night. Using the headlights of their vehicle to spot deer provided a few tactical advantages over the use of a spotlight. Since every vehicle utilized headlights at night it did not draw the attention of a spotlight. In addition, a spotlight could be seen for miles on a clear night. Furthermore, a driver using their headlights could turn into a field, illuminating it, and back out and go back in the direction from which they had come and if stopped they could claim they were merely turning around and not intentionally shining the field. While this defense normally did not work, it could be viewed as a legitimate excuse for lighting up a field.

However, when they turned in and shined a field and then continued in the direction they were headed they lost this "defense" since it isn't a normal part of driving to turn off the road and shine an area.

Having observed this furtive activity, the officer had stopped the vehicle. There he found five young men and one loaded .22-caliber rifle in the back seat. Although five was a lot of folks to be together night hunting, the setup was a typical one in that the group only had one gun. In addition, .22-caliber rifles were used widely by folks hunting at night partially because of their low report versus that of a high-powered rifle. I advised Greg it sounded like a good case; however, like with all cases, it would be stronger with a confession and I suggested we read the folks their rights and take their statements.

I took the handcuffed driver to our vehicle to talk with him. As I began to read the young man the Miranda warning he asked if I could please take the handcuffs off seeing how he was having trouble feeling his hands. I checked the cuffs and found they were snug but not overly tight. However, I was thinking seeing how everything was under control and I did not sense any threat from this individual and he had been wearing the bracelets for over an hour, it would be a goodwill gesture to remove the cuffs and I did. I read him the warning and asked him to tell me what had occurred. He stated they were just out riding around when the officer stopped them. I asked why he had turned his vehicle crossways in the road and he stated a deer had run across the road and he was trying to get a look at it. When I asked who had the firearm he said it was in the back of the SUV. I asked if he was night hunting and he assured me he was not. I told him to sit tight and we would be back with him.

I moved to the next subject and basically went through the same scenario. I received a very similar story. I realized that in his excitement of making his first night hunting case by himself, the new officer had forgotten the rule about separating the folks involved to prevent them from getting their stories together. However, reading this individual's body language I could tell something was amiss so I pressed forward. I informed the man I had been told he was in possession of the firearm when the vehicle had been stopped. He stammered around and said the front seat passenger had slid the rifle back to him when the officer had pulled them over. I asked why he thought they had the rifle and he did not answer. I asked if it was his rifle and he answered with an emphatic "No." A good technique any time you had multiple subjects was to ask whether or not the gun belonged to them. If it did you had another strike against them and another set of questions to ask. If it did not belong to them that told you something as well. I played up the fact this guy was in possession of the gun and again asked what their intent was. He advised he was along for the ride. I gave him my best "I know you're lying" look and again inquired as to what he thought the front-seat passenger's intentions were and he finally said, "To shoot a deer."

Armed with this new information I returned to the driver. This time my tone was more accusatory and I asked him a simple question that had worked for me many times: "Is there any reason why what you said and what your buddy told me are two totally different stories?" This often worked to jar loose the truth. I followed with the quick question, "Was the firearm in the front seat prior to you getting stopped?" Seeing things were going downhill, the fellow hung his head. That was normally a good sign. The guy looked up at me with the "What have I done?" look and I knew we had him. I told him to just go ahead and tell it. He stated they had been out riding around hoping to see a deer. He said he wasn't sure they would have shot it but they might have. That was good enough for me. I gave him a pen and a piece of paper and asked him to write out his statement. We did the same with the other four individuals and the results were pretty much the same. Greg issued citations for hunting at night, hunting from a public road, and hunting by the aid of a vehicle. That was a lot of tickets.

The court date soon rolled around and I was about to receive a rude awakening. The cases were called and the five defendants and three officers approached the bench. I got a bad feeling as soon as the judge asked the defendants, "What are you boys doing in here?" I was thinking that was pretty obvious seeing the charges on the docket. The judge looked at CEO Gilliland and asked why he had brought these boys to court. Greg testified he had observed as an SUV moved slowly along the road and turned and illuminated a field with its headlights. The driver backed out and continued the same way it had been going. He stopped the vehicle and found a loaded rifle in the back seat. He finished his testimony by saying after having been read their rights the defendants had given a written confession stating they were night hunting. I felt the young officer had done a good job and waited to hear the response of the defendants. However, I didn't get to hear it. In a normal court proceeding the judge would listen to our reason for bringing the charges and then ask the defendant for their side of the story. That didn't happen. Instead the judge thought for a minute and announced he didn't think that was what these boys were doing. My blood pressure immediately jumped at least fifty points! I'm sure you could have taken my pulse by looking at my neck from across the room. As the senior officer of the group I stepped up to the bench and informed the judge we had a signed confession that stated they were night hunting. The judge gave me a disparaging look that made it obvious he wasn't interested in anything I had to say and announced he would take the cases under advisement. That was normally judicial code for "This case is going away!"

I wanted to jump up and grab the judge by his scrawny neck. I had been told he was no friend of conservation; however, I never thought we would lose such a slam-dunk case. Unfortunately, this went on for years. I felt so sorry for the officers who had to work in that jurisdiction on a regular basis. One day was just about more than I could take.

Unfortunately, there are many judges who have little regard for the peril of our wildlife resources much less the fact that CEOs put their lives on the line to protect those resources and the public. When these lawbreakers are let go with a slap on the wrist or less, it perpetuates the idea that wildlife is of little value. As I said at the start, I am so thankful I had good conservation-minded judges. Knowing this sure helped when it was seven degrees at 2:00 a.m. in the middle of nowhere and it was just you against them!

SLOW LEARNERS
WITH SHORT MEMORIES

BELIEVE IT OR NOT listening to the police radio is a skill that has to be honed. I'm not referring to the codes that are used. What is needed is the skill to recognize what is relevant to you. That isn't difficult when you only have one channel. However, almost every law enforcement vehicle is equipped with a radio that scans numerous frequencies. This is necessary so you know what is happening around you. Unfortunately, it is not uncommon to have more than one department that is experiencing a high-priority call at the same time. While you are trying to decipher what is happening with them, you also have to be listening for your own calls. It can definitely get confusing.

Being in our small county with few officers working, I often try to monitor the radio even when I'm off duty. There are many times when there is only one officer working and you never know when someone may need some assistance. While listening, I heard a deputy call in to dispatch that he was making a traffic stop. In a moment, he called in the driver's license number. The dispatcher stated the license came back to Mr. Lim Do. After a couple of minutes, the deputy stated he was back in service after issuing a citation for speeding (eighty-four in a fifty-five).

Approximately five minutes later I heard another deputy, the patrol sergeant at the time, report he was making a traffic stop. He gave the tag number and I immediately realized it was the same tag the other deputy had just stopped. I probably need to tell you I have a thing about numbers and could usually remember tag numbers and driver's license numbers for a long time. The dispatcher responded to the officer it was in fact the same vehicle the other deputy had just stopped. The sergeant came back on the radio with a classic line, he replied "Must be a slow learner." In just a couple of minutes he radioed he was back in service after issuing a citation for speeding (seventy-two in a fifty-five). I later spoke with the sergeant about the stop and he said the driver never said a word about receiving a ticket just five minutes earlier.

Fast forward maybe five years. I am working with a deputy and we clock a vehicle running eighty miles per hour in a sixty-five zone. I call the tag in to dispatch and the other deputy on shift comes on the radio and says, "I guess the ticket I just wrote him for eighty-three in a sixty-five didn't do any good." We stop the car and write the driver a speeding ticket. He never mentioned receiving one five minutes earlier.

The man came to court and was found guilty and appealed his cases to circuit court. His argument was there was only like three miles between the places he was stopped and there was no way he could get up that much speed in that amount of distance. Interestingly, the judge didn't see it that way! I wasn't sure but I swear I heard someone mumble, "What an idiot."

THAT DIDN'T HAPPEN

IN MANY PREVIOUS STORIES, I have discussed how helpful it was to receive good information from the public. There is no substitute for it. When you are trying to cover hundreds of square miles it is a blessing to receive accurate information that allows you to zero in on a small area to work.

Unfortunately, for all the good information we received, we would receive much more that was not so good. While I believe it was only a few folks who would purposefully provide erroneous or misleading information, many were prone to exaggerate and sometimes even fabricate things. All information had to be evaluated based on what we knew and the feeling we got when we were receiving it.

I remember an incident where my partner, Hershel Patterson, and I were speaking with an individual who was complaining about all the night hunting of deer occurring around his area. Hershel assured the man he had been working the area but had not encountered any night hunters. The fellow acted as if he did not hear a word Hershel said and continued to complain saying, "Just last night someone shot in the kudzu patch just west of my house." Hershel asked the man what time that occurred and "eight thirty" was his quick reply. Hershel quickly replied, "That didn't happen." I must admit his quick and terse response took me a little by surprise.

The man immediately went on the offensive and stated in no uncertain terms he guessed it did happen because his brother who lived across from the kudzu patch told him he heard the shot. "Not at eight thirty he didn't," was Hershel's solemn reply. Now the man was really on the defensive and said there was no reason his brother would lie about it. Hershel said, "He must have been mistaken." The irritated man shot back, "How do you know?" and Hershel quickly answered, "Because I was sitting in that kudzu patch from seven until midnight and no one shot in it or anywhere close by it!" The man was now wearing a bewildered look and said, "Well it must have been some other night."

I came to believe many people erroneously believed if they would exaggerate their report they might get a better response. The story of the boy who cried wolf comes to mind. I learned fairly early on when someone reported they were hearing shooting every night it normally wasn't true. In addition, when folks would report night hunters had shot five or six or ten times, it normally wasn't night hunting. There were a few exceptions to that. One was if the shooter was using a .22-caliber rifle. In my experience, night hunters who used a .22 rifle were normally good shots and made head shots on deer. However, I have had night hunters who used a .22 to shoot several times. Another exception was when someone was shooting with a semi-automatic handgun. Yes, I had that happen, more than once.

I received a call one night from the Sheriff's Office (SO) dispatch saying Mr. Ficquette had reported someone had just shot east of his house on Coosa County Road 4. He said they had shot multiple times with a .22 rifle and left going east toward Highway 9. This was not Mr. Ficquette's first rodeo. His area held a lot of deer and having someone shoot at them at night was far too common. When he observed the slow-moving vehicle pass by his house, he immediately went and got in his vehicle. When they shot he took off toward them and was able to get a vehicle description complete with tag number.

As a general rule we always asked landowners not to chase night hunters. While we understood how aggravating it was to have some thug shooting near your home, we also knew that in the event a landowner was able to overtake a night hunter there could be a deadly confrontation. Of course, we could not stop landowners from chasing folks but we requested they call us instead. In this case the homeowner had done things right. He did not try to stop the vehicle but did get a good description. He also immediately had called the SO and asked them to call us.

I asked the dispatcher to put out a BOLO (be on the lookout) for the vehicle and I headed toward the Ficquette residence. I met the homeowner on the road where the shooting had taken place and located seven spent .22 cartridges. As I was gathering the information, the SO dispatch called and advised a state trooper had the vehicle stopped at Highway 280. She went on to say the trooper advised it contained two teenagers and two .22 rifles. I asked her to have him separate them and advise I was en route.

I hurriedly made my way to up Highway 9 to Highway 280. The vehicle matched the description given by the landowner. I spoke with the trooper and he told me he had the rifles in his trunk and he had smelled them and they had not been fired. I immediately asked him if he had shared that information with the teenagers and he said he had. I was ready to hit top limb. While I knew that the trooper's estimation that the guns had not been fired had no valid weight as he was not a firearms expert, I knew it would definitely be a hurdle I had to get over in court. I showed him the handful of spent cartridges and told him the landowner had watched them shoot. He had a dumbfounded look on his face.

THAT DIDN'T HAPPEN

I moved to the violators and ascertained what information I could. They quickly told me the trooper had checked their guns and stated they had not been fired. I replied, "He was wrong, wasn't he?" They decided they did not want to say anything else. I gathered their information and allowed them to go on their way sans guns.

I went back and took a detailed statement from Mr. Ficquette. He assured me he would be ready to testify in court if necessary. I told him it might very well be necessary. The two teens were charged with hunting at night, hunting from a public road, and hunting by the aid of a vehicle.

The next month I entered the courtroom and was immediately approached by an attorney who told me he represented the two youths. He was very quick to tell me the trooper had checked the guns and stated they had not been fired. Although this was a discussion our assistant district attorney (ADA) should have been in, he was not in the courtroom so I moved forward. I advised the attorney I did not know whether or not he planned to call the trooper to testify but if he did I would challenge whether or not he was a firearms expert qualified to make that determination simply by smelling a gun. I told him I did have an eyewitness that had observed the incident and was eager to testify that the individuals in the vehicle had fired multiple shots very near his home. The fellow just smiled at me and walked away.

Eventually the ADA showed up and the attorney quickly approached him. Fortunately, things went like I thought they would in that the ADA looked at the case file and then pointed at me and told the attorney to talk to me about it. The attorney knew my position so this time he approached with his hat in his hand so to speak and asked if we could work something out. Knowing the hurdle I had to get over I felt I probably should get what I could. I told the counselor if his clients wanted to plead guilty to the hunting at night I would request the other charges be dismissed. He consulted with his clients and gave me a thumbs up.

While we did not encourage landowners to chase night hunters, this was one instance in which I was really glad they did. Had I not had the landowner's testimony, I would have been hard-pressed to have won the cases. I appreciated good information.

I later put together a presentation I offered to various police departments and sheriff's offices in an effort to help them understand the elements of our cases and what we needed from them in the event they encountered someone they felt had violated some of our laws and/or regulations. It contained a lot of information, including "don't be smelling any gun barrels!"

SHHH!
(BE VERY QUIET)

As the young boy looked back at him, the officer placed his index finger to his lips in the universal "keep quiet" or "shhh" symbol. The boy dutifully remained silent. The officer had witnessed a lot in his career but couldn't believe what was unfolding before him.

I have penned many stories concerning trying to apprehend people who were hunting by the aid of bait. Although it was illegal to hunt wildlife by the aid of bait for most of my career, the practice was rampant all across the state. Even after the rules were loosened to allow hunting near a feeding station as long as it was one hundred yards away and out of the line of sight, multitudes continued to sit watching a bait pile during the deer season. You know baiting is rampant when convenience stores move beer displays to make room for pallets of bags of deer corn. I kid you not!

Conservation Enforcement Officer (CEO) Lt. Jerry Fincher had learned of an area where corn had been placed in order to lure deer in and had checked the area several times but had yet to find anyone hunting the area. Every time a CEO checks a baited site the chances of being spotted increase. It often seemed the woods had eyes and after the game camera explosion the woods basically did have eyes.

This baited area was located where there was nowhere nearby to hide a truck. Therefore, Jerry needed someone to drop him on the location and come and pick him up later. This task usually fell on his partner; however, it wasn't unusual for officers to enlist the assistance of officers from other departments, trusted landowners, and, as happened in this case, their wives.

As I was working as the private lands biologist for all of south Alabama, it was difficult for me to find time to do much enforcement work. However, I finally managed to save a few hours and went to work with Jerry. He asked me to drop him on the baited site. He explained in an effort to avoid detection he was taking an extended route to get to the location. He stated while the bait was poured out in a low area, there was a ground blind on a fairly high hill overlooking it. He had checked the blind several times without finding anyone and today was no different. As always, after you had worked a place numerous times you feared you may have been spotted. However, as a general rule as long as they continued to add to the corn we would keep checking it.

A couple of weeks later I received a call from Jerry stating he had caught someone over the bait and I would not believe the story. I said, "Try me." I knew I had amassed numerous unbelievable stories and Jerry was developing a long list as well. This was a good one. His wife had dropped him out near the site and he hurriedly made his way toward the bait. As he came upon a woods roads intersection he observed a green backpack sitting on the ground. He felt this indicated there was obviously someone in the area and he crossed his fingers in hopes this would be the day he caught someone on the bait. Just about as fast as he had seen a glimmer of hope, the rug was pulled out from under his feet.

When he reached the backpack and looked up the road in the direction of the ground blind, there stood a man and a young boy looking directly at him. Take it from me, getting caught in this type of situation was agonizing. You had put in so much effort just to see it all circling the drain. It felt like a strong kick below the belt. You had spent a lot of time initially locating the bait. You had made numerous trips to the site doing your best not to be detected and now the many hours invested were for naught.

Dejected the officer started toward the pair. He had immediately noticed they neither one were wearing any hunter orange. It was bad enough the adult did not have any orange on but it was worse that he had brought the young boy to the woods without any. The officer would address the situation.

When he was within thirty feet of the pair the man turned and started walking toward the baited area. Baffled, Jerry did not understand exactly what was going on. As he watched, the man assumed a stalking posture with the young boy directly behind him. The boy turned and looked at Jerry who was in uniform and wearing his orange hat. The officer put his index finger to his lips and gently shook his head from side to side. The boy repeatedly looked back as they moved up the hill. Soon they reached the top of the hill. The father put his hand out and stopped the boy. The boy again turned to face the officer who gave him the "shhh" sign. The father then crept up over the lip of the hill so he could check and see if there was anything standing in the corn pile. When he turned back toward his son he was taken aback when he was face to face with a game warden who whispered, "Is there anything down there?" The man now wore a bewildered look on his face. Jerry took his gun and asked to see his license.

As he wrote the man a ticket for hunting by the aid of bait and hunting without wearing hunter orange he could not help but ask if the man had not seen him as he came up to the intersection. The man replied he had seen him but since there were four other people hunting the property he thought he was one of them. Hey, every once in a while, things went our way. You can't make this stuff up!

280 BALLGAME TRAFFIC
(NOT MY FAVORITE)

I WOULD ASSUME all law enforcement officers have a favorite and least favorite area and time to work. I have written several stories of my favorite places to work. One of my least favorite places to work was US Highway 280, which cuts through Coosa County. The highway is a straight shot from Birmingham to Auburn. On days of, prior to, and after an Auburn football game the highway was somewhere I did not want to be. Just trying to cross the road in the evening after a game was a nightmare. Most law enforcement did their best not to be on the road. Experience had taught us the traffic normally flowed better if we stayed out of the way. Of course, that wasn't always possible. Working with the Coosa County Sheriff's Office deputies, I worked the traffic on occasion. It wasn't fun but it was often eventful.

I remember one afternoon Deputy Shane House and I were patrolling the highway on a Saturday afternoon. It was early in the evening and a few hours prior to the onslaught of traffic that would arrive after the ballgame. We noticed a Jeep that appeared to be moving at a high rate of speed. Shane activated the radar and it showed the vehicle was traveling at eighty-two miles per hour. We crossed the median and came up behind the fast-moving vehicle. Shane activated our blue lights and the driver pulled to the side of the road. We approached the vehicle, which was driven by a middle-aged woman. The back seat was occupied by a small dog.

Shane advised the driver our radar had indicated she was traveling at eighty-two miles per hour and asked the lady for her driver's license and proof of insurance. She replied she was in a hurry because she had to take her dog to the emergency vet in Birmingham. Shane again asked to see her license and proof of insurance. With a huff she started digging for her license. I had eased up to the passenger side of the vehicle and had noticed a half-full bottle of wine in the passenger seat. As the woman looked for her license, I got Shane's attention and pointed to the bottle. The woman continued to look for her license and at the same time reiterated she didn't have time for this since she needed to get her dog to the vet. Shane asked what was wrong with her dog and she replied she could tell the dog didn't feel well. While we obviously weren't familiar with the dog, it appeared fine to us. It was lying on the back seat with its head up and did not appear to be in any type of distress.

The woman finally handed Shane her license and he asked her to step out of the vehicle. She again stated she didn't have time for this. He told her again she needed to step out of the vehicle.

I learned a long time ago that watching someone you suspected of being under the influence as they exited their vehicle often told the tale as to whether or not they were in fact intoxicated. That held true in this instance as well. The woman had trouble exiting the vehicle and was very unstable as she moved to the rear of it. Shane asked how much she had had to drink and she replied she had not had anything. He mentioned the open container in her front seat and she replied, "That's just wine!" He told her he would like for her to take some tests to make sure she was okay to drive. The woman seemed to be disgusted with us messing up her day. However, she only thought her day had been messed up! Her next statement really put a kink in things when she asked, "Would a hundred dollars make all of this go away?"

I'm sure my face had an astonished "Did I just hear that?" look on it. I know that because that was the look on Shane's face. Shane quickly handcuffed the woman who was now wearing an astonished look on her face. I wasn't sure whether her look was saying she couldn't believe her offer didn't work or she couldn't believe she was now in handcuffs on the side of the road! As often happens, the woman was now very cooperative and willing to take the tests. Shane advised her she was under arrest for bribery and asked her if there was someone who could come and get her dog. The woman now looked as though she was in a state of shock. Shane again asked if she had someone to come and get her dog. The woman finally replied her husband could come and get it. We contacted the husband and advised him of the situation and he said he would be en route. We had another unit come and stay with the dog while we transported the woman to the jail.

The next month she appeared in court with her attorney. As I recall, they offered to plead to the DUI if we would drop the bribery charge. Seeing how we had the one-hundred-dollar offer on video, we countered that she could plead to all of it. She was found guilty.

I have often wondered due to the nonchalant way she offered to pay her way out of the situation if that was the first time she had tried that. I'll never know; however, I would be surprised if she is so quick to try it again!

On yet another game day Shane and I had been patrolling in the county and staying away from Highway 280. However, around midnight we decided to venture that way. Normally by that time, traffic had receded to a workable level. We were traveling eastbound and soon observed a car moving at a high rate of speed. Our radar indicated the driver was driving at 115 miles per hour.

We quickly cut through the median and began pursuing the vehicle with our lights and siren activated. While it took a minute to catch up to the vehicle we were soon right behind the fleeing driver. Fortunately, the driver began to slow down and pulled to the right side of the road. I mentioned earlier about watching for cues from a driver when you had them get out of the vehicle; well, you obviously also watch the driver prior to them stopping. In this instance, the driver pulled to the side of the road and hit the guard rail, raking it down the side of his vehicle.

We exited our vehicle and approached the driver, the only occupant in the vehicle. Shane told the young man to exit the vehicle. He got out and steadied himself on the vehicle as he walked to the rear. We asked for his driver's license and he produced it. His license showed he was nineteen years old. Shane asked how much he had had to drink. At that point the fellow went berserk! He began screaming profanities and saying why couldn't we just leave him alone. Shane told the young fellow he needed to calm down, which brought on another blue streak of cussing. Interestingly, this tirade ended with him saying he had already gotten one ticket and we could just write him another one. Shane asked where the ticket was and the young man pulled the crumpled piece of paper from his pocket and thrust it at the officer. The ticket had been issued by a municipality about thirty miles east of where we were now. It was for speeding. Ninety-six miles per hour in a sixty-five-mile-per-hour zone!

Shane administered a couple of field sobriety tests, which the teenager failed miserably. We placed the young man under arrest and transported him to jail. While the blood alcohol limit (BAC) is .08 for adults, for folks under twenty-one years of age the limit is .02. This fellow's BAC was .22. Eleven times the legal limit!

Interestingly, we received a letter from the young man in which he thanked us for saving his life. In addition, we met his parents, who also thanked us for saving their son. I have no way of knowing where that man is now, but I hope he really did learn his lesson and turned his life around.

On yet another occasion I had an interesting encounter that was spawned by an Auburn football game. I was driving west bound on Highway 280 in Alexander City when I was passed by a small car traveling at a very high rate of speed. Although working traffic was not something game and fish often did, we sometimes made exceptions when we felt it was necessary for safety. I guess the fact I could not even see anyone in the driver's seat of this car made me think I might should investigate what was going on. Although it took me a little distance to catch up with the vehicle, I eventually pulled in behind the car and activated my blue lights. You never knew how a driver was going to react and I definitely wasn't expecting what happened next. As soon as I activated my blue lights, the driver locked the car's brakes down and slid to a stop in the highway! I had to pull onto the shoulder of the road to keep from colliding with the vehicle. Seeing how I was now side by side with the car, I motioned for the driver to pull in front of me on the side of the highway.

I exited my Tahoe and walked up to the driver's window. Looking inside I initially felt I knew what the problem was. Twelve-year-old kids should not be driving. I asked the little girl for her driver's license and was surprised when she handed it to me. The license revealed the girl was in fact nineteen years old. It also showed she was four feet nine inches and weighed a whopping eighty-two pounds!

I regained my composure and asked why the young girl was in such a hurry. It did not escape me that she was wearing what appeared to be pajamas. She said she was just trying to get home. She went on to say she had been to the ballgame on Saturday and was just now headed home. I reasoned that if I was nineteen years old and had been to a ballgame that ended forty-eight hours earlier and was driving wearing my pajamas, I would probably be in a hurry to get home as well! I advised her she needed to slow down and drive more safely. While working traffic on 280 produced some interesting stories, I'd rather stick with game and fish!

STARGAZERS
(THE DARKEST PLACE IN ALABAMA)

ALTHOUGH I KNEW the doctor would easily pay the hefty fine and would probably be released by the end of the day, I also knew he would never forget the humility of being walked to the jail in handcuffs. A good rule of thumb is to remember the district court judge is a resident of the county he serves and where your crime took place; therefore, ticking him off by trashing the county residents is probably not a wise move.

The Coosa Wildlife Management Area (WMA) encompassed 38,000 contiguous acres on the western boundary of Coosa County. The vast majority of the area was remote to say the least. With the exception of a few cabins on the lake and the WMA workshop, there were no houses or developments on the area. The remote location and absence of lighting were the factors that led to the recognition of the area as the darkest place in Alabama. This designation meant the area was a favorite for astronomers. As a matter of fact, at one time, the area was supposedly listed on a NASA website as the quintessential stargazing location in the state. This had prompted the Birmingham Astronomy Club to post directions to the area on their website and generated a lot of nighttime visitation.

Normally folks who were into astronomy were not the type of people that caused the normal problems on the WMA. However,

I'm sure you have heard there's an exception to every rule. Well, it was only a matter of time until I ran into the exception.

I received a call from an amateur astronomer who regularly used the area to stargaze. His concern was someone he described as being from the Birmingham group had cut several trees that had grown to the point they were disrupting the view at a favorite viewing spot. He knew cutting trees on the WMA, which was owned in large part by a paper company whose primary goal was growing trees, was illegal and would not go over very well. He wanted me to know he didn't have anything to do with the tree cutting. I told him I appreciated the info and would go and check out the situation.

At my next opportunity, I located the site and sure enough someone had cut the tops out of about one hundred pine trees surrounding an old log landing where the people had been setting up their telescopes. A few weeks went by and I received another phone call concerning the group. This caller advised he had been on the WMA on Saturday night and was confronted by a man with a gun who told him to get out of the area. I asked exactly where this had occurred and he described the very location where the trees had been topped. Now things had gotten much more serious.

I placed a call to someone I thought would probably have some info concerning the group. Developing contacts who have their finger on the pulse of various activities is essential to being able to effectively police your area of responsibility. One call to someone who is "in the know" can save you days of investigation. My contact explained the fellow who was primarily using the site was a medical doctor from Birmingham who owned the largest privately owned telescope in the state. It was his understanding the doctor had been taking groups to the site and had been "providing security" for them by threatening people with his assault rifle topped with a night vision scope!

It was apparent this had to be addressed so I contacted my fellow wildlife biologist, Gene Carver, and asked if he would accompany me to do a little observation of our own. I explained the ordeal and Gene agreed to come over and assist. I had information the individual would likely be on the area on Saturday night, weather permitting, so we made plans to make his acquaintance.

Saturday evening Gene and I were patrolling the Ridge Road on the WMA. The ridge road was the main artery on the north side of the WMA. It was several miles long and ran all the way to the Coosa River. With approximately two hundred miles of road, there was no shortage of areas to work on the WMA.

We waited until about 8:00 p.m. to go and check out the observation point. As we neared the area, we could see there were fresh tire tracks leading into the opening. We turned down the dim road and made our way to the opening. As we approached we saw there were several vehicles parked in the area. We pulled up behind the closest vehicle and I implemented our high-tech safety plan. I purposely left our headlights on bright to hopefully disable the night vision scope on the rifle the individual was supposed to possess. We put a lot of thought into that!

We quickly exited our truck and moved off to the side of the road. Immediately we saw a man approaching the truck and he called out to us, "Who goes there?" I replied, "State game warden," and turned my flashlight on and pointed it toward the source of the question. There stood a man holding what appeared to be an assault-style rifle with a scope. As my light illuminated the man, his rifle evidently became quite hot and he immediately dropped the gun to the ground and began walking toward me as if to make conversation. In an unmistakable tone, I told the man to stay where he was and raise his hands over his head. Dealing with one armed subject was bad enough, but adding ten more people to the mix really raised the stakes. Gene lit up the other people with his light and had them raise their hands as well. As I covered the man, Gene moved over and retrieved the rifle. We moved everyone toward the front of my truck where we could see them. I asked if anyone else had any weapons on their person and they all replied they did not. We asked about weapons in vehicles and two of the individuals told us they had handguns in their vehicles. We retrieved those guns.

During the time we were making things secure, the lead individual had done his best to carry on a conversation with us as if he was our best buddy. This wasn't that easy as he was face down and being handcuffed. However, it was not unusual conduct for someone who knew they were in trouble. With all of the weapons unloaded and in my truck, it was time to talk to the owner of the rifle.

The first thing I did was read him the Miranda warning. He acted as if this was the first time anything had ever happened to him and I felt it probably was. He stated he understood his rights. He started into his story of how he was only trying to protect himself and others. I stopped him and asked if he knew he was on the Coosa WMA. He affirmed he did. I asked if he was aware there were numerous rules and regulations that pertained to users of the area. He stated he wasn't really aware of that. I told him that was unfortunate since one of the rules was you could not possess a firearm on the WMA and he was under arrest for violation of that regulation. This revelation seemed to diminish his longing for a conversation and he didn't offer a lot after that.

While Gene was talking with the remainder of the group, I questioned the good doctor about how often he had visited this site. He stated he had used the site several times since it was one of the darkest places in Alabama. This answer verified he had traveled into the area multiple times, passing a multitude of bright yellow signs indicating special rules and regulations applied on the area. It also confirmed for me he had either cut the trees or had them cut to improve his view. I asked if he knew who had cut the trees on the site. He assured me he didn't know who had done that. I felt certain he had done it but it wasn't anything I could prove so I let it go. I took his driver's license and began writing him a ticket.

I finished with the ticket and informed the doctor I was going to allow him to sign his bond and would not take him to jail. This seemed to lighten his mood considerably. We completed the paperwork and he invited us to look through his telescope which he informed us was the largest privately owned scope in the state. It was impressive. As I recall it had a thirty-six-inch barrel and was about ten feet tall. You had to climb a ladder to look through it. We briefly looked at the scope. Gene had ascertained the remainder of the group were all guests of the gun-wielding doctor and had no idea they were violating any laws. We explained the applicable rules and regulations to the guests and we told them we felt they had not intentionally committed any violations. Therefore, we issued verbal warnings. Feeling we had sufficiently embarrassed their host, we left the scene.

The next month the doctor appeared before the judge in Coosa County district court. The case was called and the defendant, Gene, and I approached the bench. The judge read the charge of possession of a firearm without a permit on the WMA and asked the defendant what his plea was. The defendant stammered around and said he didn't know you could not have a weapon. The judge said he was going to consider that a not guilty and told us to raise our hands and be sworn. He asked me to tell him what had occurred. I explained that in response to complaints of WMA users being threatened by a man with a rifle, we had gone to the area. Upon our arrival, we were confronted by the defendant, who was in fact in possession of an assault-style rifle fitted with a night vision scope. I told him the man had no permit to possess the weapon on the WMA and was arrested. The judge looked at Gene and asked if he had anything to add. I had learned early on that Gene had a knack for saying just the right thing to make the judge want to throw the book at a defendant. I had seen this happen several times and today was no exception. Gene made a comment to the effect of the defendant was from Birmingham and he felt he was imitating Rambo, an action movie figure of the time, in an effort to impress a group of out-of-towners he had brought to the site.

Having worked with the judge for many years, I knew he was basically unpredictable except for when he began breathing hard through his nose. When that started happening, things were going to get rough for someone. This was usually, but not always, the defendant. In this case it was. The judge turned to the defendant and while breathing hard asked if he had anything to say. The doctor replied he had carried the gun for protection because he did not know "what kind of people were down here" and didn't know who might be out there. The "people down here" comment from a Birmingham city dweller to a lifelong county resident judge went over like a turd in a punch bowl!

The judge began scribbling in the case file and through clenched teeth told the defendant the court found him guilty and sentenced him to a $500 fine and thirty days to serve in jail! The dumbfounded defendant was staring at the judge with a slack jaw as the judge said, "You are in the custody of the sheriff." The defendant looked at me and asked, "Should I get an attorney?" I replied, "It's a little late for that, but you will be allowed to a make a call from the jail." With that, a deputy took him by the arm and led him to the holding box. Five hundred dollars was a hefty fine for a management area violation; however, it proved you just didn't know what kind of people you might run into down here! Obviously, the judge wanted to get his attention.

After this incident, I never saw another stargazer in the area. The directions to the WMA were removed from the club's website and things were back to normal. Interestingly, about ten years after that incident, I had the opportunity to meet a guy on some private property near my home. He was a member of a hunting club on a property adjacent to my hunting lease. While planting some wildlife openings, a friend and I had met the guy on the road leading to his club and got into a conversation. When he learned of my profession, he commented he had had an interesting encounter with a couple of game wardens on the management area one night. He went on to relay the story of how he and his wife were invited to go and do some stargazing through a large telescope that a doctor in Birmingham owned. I listened as he related each detail of the case and was a little surprised that he told it just as it had happened. He finished by saying the officers had given him a warning for having a handgun in his vehicle and they had written the owner of the scope a ticket. He said he didn't know what had ever come of the case. I asked what he thought about the whole situation and he stated he felt like the wardens had done just what they should have and he wouldn't want a job where you had to walk up on a nut with an assault rifle. After receiving his assessment of our conduct, I asked if he would like to know the outcome of the case. He looked at me with a puzzled look on his face and then asked, "Was that you?" I replied it was and told him what had occurred in court. To which he responded, "That's just what he deserved."

It wasn't often you got to hear a true unbiased critique of your performance. I appreciated his comments and felt good that he, having been there, felt justice had been served. Although the judge later dropped the thirty days of jail time and I'm sure the

$500 plus court costs was nothing to the doctor, I have the feeling he will probably never forget the night he made our acquaintance and the day he met the county judge in the darkest place in Alabama.

CALL THE POLICE!

WORKING WITH THE PUBLIC, especially in a law enforcement capacity, brought you together with a bunch of interesting characters. Although some of these folks were such that would break any law they could, they were sometimes still likeable types. I was pretty familiar with such a fellow who I had the opportunity to "meet" on multiple occasions. On one of our meetings, he told me a story that definitely falls into the "you can't make this stuff up" category!

It seems the fellow was driving down Fort Williams Street in Sylacauga in Talladega County late one night when he noticed a vehicle behind him whose driver was acting erratically. He explained the car would run right up to his bumper and then back off and then do it again. He said he did not recognize the car as belonging to anyone he knew. When the car ran up on him again, he decided he would see what was going on. He said he had a heavy-duty bumper hitch on the rear of his four-wheel-drive pickup and he felt it would probably match up pretty good with the grill of the car behind him. Therefore, when the vehicle came running up on him again, he slammed on the brakes and sure enough his bumper ball went right through the grill and into the radiator of the car.

CALL THE POLICE!

He jumped out of the truck and ran back to the car to find the driver retrieving a shotgun from the passenger's seat and sticking it out the window. He said he grabbed the gun by the barrel and pulled it away from the driver who he recognized as a man who was dating his ex-girlfriend. He said he pitched the gun to the ground and then proceeded to pull the man out through the car window. When the man swung his fist at him he blocked the blow and then made short work of the man, beating him severely.

He nonchalantly told me that with the driver bloodied and beaten and lying in the road, he decided he needed to call the police to come and work the accident. He said he gathered up the shotgun, to keep the man from trying to use it again, and walked to a nearby house to ask them to call the police. This was before everyone had a cell phone. He said it was near midnight when he knocked on the door.

Eventually a woman opened the door and, although he didn't have an opportunity to say anything, at the sight of a man covered in blood and holding a shotgun, she immediately began screaming and slammed the door shut. He said he was a little startled by her response but just hollered for her to call the police. I was thinking that request probably wasn't necessary!

He said in just a couple of minutes the police showed up. He explained how there had been a traffic accident and how the driver who had run into him had tried to shoot him with a shotgun. A fight had ensued and he had been able to subdue the driver. He said they had a few questions for him and then he was allowed to leave.

I think the thing that caught my attention was how matter-of-factly he told the whole story. Just like it was something that happened every day.

Believe me when I tell you I experienced a lot of episodes and heard a lot of stories that you just couldn't make up!

SHOOTING FROM THE PORCH

YEARS AGO, before baiting for deer was legalized, we spent a lot of time looking for baited areas. You might be surprised to learn what all people used for bait. Of course, the most common bait was corn. However, many folks tried a lot of different baits. Everything from cottonseed to apples and pears, and even peanut butter, were often used. I honestly believe many hunters would try anything they heard might work.

Not only was the bait interesting, so was the way it was delivered. I want to believe I have seen most ways of bait delivery. While you always had those who would simply pour feed out on the ground, others would use some type of feeder. While most folks used what I would call a normal feeder, some not-so-normal ones were also employed. Through my career I witnessed a progression of feeders. Early on the commercial feeders were basically a five-gallon bucket with a hole in the bottom. Then a stick was added and animals touching the stick made the feed fall out. Later a spinner was attached to the bottom of the bucket to sling the feed out.

Other folks would in effect use a trough-type feeder. These varied greatly in design. I remember one deer season when I received some information concerning a feeder sitting out in front of a small cabin. I made my way to the property and easily located the fifty-five-gallon plastic barrel that had been cut in half longways and placed about forty yards in front of the cabin. This was before there was a camera on every tree. I checked the barrel and found it was nearly full of corn. I took a sample of the corn and headed out of the area. I noticed there was a chair on the porch and I surmised that it would be pretty easy to hunt over the corn from the porch.

I made plans to work the area the following weekend. The plan was easy enough; however, the only problem was someone on the porch would see me approaching from a pretty good distance, which would give them time to place their gun in the cabin, possibly without me seeing it. I devised a plan I hoped would work.

The next Saturday morning, I arrived at the property at seven in the morning. I parked at the gate and noted there were fresh tracks going into the place. I put my plan into play. I donned my camo coat and orange hat and grabbed my riot shotgun and started toward the cabin. My hope was anyone seeing me approaching would assume I was a hunter and not a game warden.

As I rounded the curve, the cabin came into view and I immediately spotted a man sitting in the chair on the porch. Fortunately, he appeared to be watching the corn feeder and didn't notice me coming down the road. Once I was pretty close, I intentionally made enough noise to get the fellow's attention. He immediately stood up and, in a not so pleasant tone, informed me I was on private property. I noticed the man was not holding a firearm. While I would be surprised if he didn't have one, it was possible he was just watching to see if anything came to the feeder with no intent to shoot anything. Not probable, but possible.

Before the fellow could launch into reading me the riot act, I informed him I was a conservation officer. This brought an immediate change in his demeanor. I noticed there was a 30-30 rifle propped beside his chair. I asked the fellow for his name and he provided it and informed me this was his cabin, and it was on his "private property." That was a perfect lead in for me and I pointed to the feeder and asked if the blue barrel with the corn in it belonged to him. He didn't waste any time informing me there was no corn in that barrel. I asked was there anyone else in the cabin and he said there was not. I asked if he would accompany me as I went and looked in the barrel. I detected a change in his confidence as he again told me the feeder was empty. I told him before I went to look in the feeder, I needed to check his rifle. He immediately informed me it was unloaded. I told him for the safety of us both I was going to check it. I picked up the rifle and worked the lever and it ejected a shell. As I was removing the other six shells, the man, who was probably in his fifties, stated, "My boys must have loaded that gun." I asked if they normally loaded his gun for him and he didn't respond. I could tell he was trying to work up a believable scenario. I laid the now empty rifle on the porch and headed toward the feeder with the now forlorn-looking man in tow.

I must admit I was not surprised to find the feeder nearly full of corn. Before the man had a chance to tell me his boys must have put that corn in there after they loaded his rifle, I advised him he was under arrest for hunting by the aid of bait. He did not offer a reply.

We returned to the cabin and I completed a ticket for hunting by the aid of bait and explained the bond procedure. I informed him of the court date and headed back to my truck.

Although he had not loaded his gun and he didn't think there was any corn in the barrel, he paid the fine prior to court!

HOLD STILL
(ANOTHER DIVINE APPOINTMENT)

ONE PART OF THE JOB as a conservation enforcement officer (CEO) was working with citizens who had come in contact with wild animals. Some of the contact they would initiate and some they did not. Early in my career our department would issue permits to possess wildlife. This resulted in people "owning" everything from raccoons to mountain lions. I have commented numerous times if folks knew what all species people had as "pets" it would curl their hair. This went far beyond indigenous wildlife species. I remember very well when someone's "pet" African lions escaped from their cages and promptly went next door and began killing the neighbor's miniature horses (you can't make this up). I digress! Suffice it to say we eventually stopped giving permits and made it illegal to possess (almost) any indigenous species. Exotics were left to the United States Department of Agriculture to handle. Of course, we still got the calls.

Despite being against the law, not to mention dangerous, many people still wanted to keep wild animals as pets. Obviously, the worst time of year for this was during the deer fawning season and unfortunately for us that might occur anytime between June and October. (As I am rereading this story in the first week of February, I have just had retired CEO Byron Smith contact me telling me he is watching a spotted fawn in a food plot!) The calls for "orphaned" fawns were common. I'm sure on some occasions they really were orphans but most of the time, as far as the public was concerned, a fawn was considered orphaned if someone was able to catch it! When we received a call from someone stating they had an orphaned fawn we would advise them to return the fawn to where they found it. That is when they would inform us they had left out the part about having seen the doe run over, or the dogs that were chasing the fawn trying to kill it, and so on. We would do our best to explain the best chance the animal had was to be released where it had been picked up. When this was met with resistance we would end up telling them if they still had it when we got to them they would be receiving a ticket. I know that sounds harsh but when you are killing hundreds of thousands of deer each year, it isn't practical to tie up a lot of resources on trying to save every one.

Deer weren't the only problem. For years in the South it had been an accepted practice to keep a raccoon as a pet. This was true even though they would normally become aggressive and mean. I almost said "as they got older," but believe me when I tell you a baby raccoon can be aggressive and mean right out of the nest! However, it was very common for folks to try to keep a raccoon and unfortunately it was common for captive raccoons to bite people. Therefore, when we got a report of someone with a raccoon we would have to investigate it and if the animal had been taken from the wild we would take it. In the event the animal had bitten or had had close contact with someone we would have to report it to the health department and have it checked for rabies.

A CEO had confiscated such a raccoon and carried it to the local vet to be put down and tested. The vet asked the officer if he would hold the animal while he gave it a shot to euthanize it. The CEO held the raccoon as the vet jabbed it with a syringe and administered the lethal drug. As the doctor removed the syringe from the raccoon he turned and inadvertently stuck the needle into the officer's arm! I can only imagine the look on the officer's face and the thoughts that immediately raced through his mind. Not only had this syringe just administered a drug lethal to a small mammal, it had just been pulled from an animal about to be tested for rabies!

Obviously, the officer kept a close watch on the wound as he waited for the rabies test results. Fortunately several of his coworkers kept in touch, asking pertinent questions such as if he had an urge to climb a tree or turn over a garbage can and rummage through its contents or maybe urinate on himself or foam at the mouth. Luckily everything turned out okay. You can't make this stuff up.

The man in this story was Conservation Enforcement Officer Senior Greg Gilliland. Greg was assigned to Talladega County, which was due north of Coosa. I worked with Greg fairly regularly. Greg's partner was Lt. Jerry Fincher, whom you've likely read about in several of my stories. Jerry was a schoolteacher prior to becoming a game warden. Ironically, my wife, Melanie, was his mentor teacher. He called her his "mother figure," which was a title he had picked up from *The Andy Griffith Show*. (If you're old enough to remember that!) I was Jerry's unofficial training officer when he became a game warden. And he was Greg's training officer. When Greg learned that Jerry called Melanie his mother figure, he decided I needed a name and he began calling me Papa Bear. He continued to do this throughout his career.

If you've read many of my stories you know that serving as a game warden can be a dangerous vocation. While everybody understands that we regularly encounter armed individuals in the middle of nowhere, they never think we might be the victim of a careless veterinarian. We take these things in stride and realize any call we respond to could be deadly. While we know that, we sometimes forget that death may visit us at any time.

I answered my phone one morning and the voice on the other end was Ginger from our district office and she said, "This is a death notification." The air immediately left my lungs. I guess those words are meant to allow you to brace yourself, although they sort of do just the opposite. I took a deep breath and asked, "Who is it?" She took a deep breath and said, "It's Greg Gilliland." I immediately broke down. I could not believe this was true. I had just seen Greg the previous week. As I cried, she continued and said, "He was riding his bicycle this morning and was ran over and killed." She apologized for having to tell me and stated she had other calls to make. I thanked her as best I could and told her I knew it wasn't an easy call to make.

My wonderful wife was sitting in the room with me and having seen my reaction to the call she was almost in tears herself. Obviously, she knew something bad had happened and was trying to brace herself for whatever was to come. I was having a difficult time holding it together. I was able to tell her that Greg had been killed and then I broke down again. Shortly, I was able to tell her what had happened.

This came as a tremendous blow to our entire department. Greg was only forty-six years old. A husband, a father, a soccer coach, a deacon in his church, and friend to all. Realizing that someone in an occupation where he knew every encounter could be his last was taken from us while riding his bicycle served as a real wakeup call. We all must be ready.

If you have read my first couple of books, you may recall they ended with a story entitled "A Divine Appointment." We all have a divine appointment that has been set for us. It is an appointment we will keep. Knowing that, we have time to make things right with the Lord. If you haven't accepted Jesus as your Lord and Savior, it's not too late. We will all spend eternity somewhere and it may be quicker than you think.

Just in case you need a little more incentive to contemplate your eternity, think about this. As I learned of Greg's death, I was awaiting a follow-up consultation with an oncologist to review the results of a skin biopsy. The week after we laid Greg to rest, I had surgery to remove melanoma and surrounding lymph nodes from my back. Today, I received a call from the doctor, who informed me that three of the four lymph nodes removed contained cancer cells. I have a scan lined up for tomorrow morning. The fact that he wanted the scan within twenty-four hours of receiving the pathology report was not lost on me. I don't know what the future holds, but I know who holds the future! I have trusted Jesus for the last fifty-four years and I'm not about to stop trusting him now. We all need to realize we are on his timetable. My dear friend Greg knew that and so do I. I hope and pray you do. Today is the day of salvation! Don't wait.

As I review this book, hopefully for the last time, I must include another update. We are at the beach with my wife's family celebrating her mother's upcoming eighty-fifth birthday. I received a call from my oncologist stating he has received my last test result and I need to get in to see him in the next two days. That didn't really sound good to me! As I sat and looked into the waves this morning, I could not get the phrase "divine appointment" out of my mind. So, I came back to this story and added this little update. I did that in the hope that if you haven't updated your life story to include Jesus, you should do it today.

As I look across the waves this morning, there is a storm rolling in. My waves are looking pretty massive. What about yours? God bless you.

EPILOGUE

Wow, what a collection of adventures. I must admit, I thoroughly enjoy reliving these situations. Well, most of them anyway. I'm once again thankful I survived them. The "He's Still Shooting" episode was likely one of the most dangerous things I ever did. It definitely had the potential to go badly. Fortunately, the Lord was once again watching over me. I have been richly blessed in many ways.

While editing this book, I received a death notice call from our district office. I was informed my good friend and fellow officer Greg Gilliland had been run over and killed while riding his bicycle. Greg worked Talladega County, which is adjacent to Coosa. Other officers have many times commented about how lucky Greg was. On more than one occasion he had pulled out of his driveway and driven up on someone night hunting or shooting from the road. He had a knack for things falling in his lap. Greg was taken much too soon at forty-six years of age. Once again, I was reminded I've lived a charmed life. I appreciate the love and support of my family and friends. My wife supports me in every endeavor and loves me despite my faults which are many.

I am truly blessed.

I will share with you that I too have faced some adversity in the past few years. I have been taking care of my previous game warden partner, Hershel Patterson, for a while now. He has been in assisted living; however, after a bout with COVID we have had to move him to the nursing home. He is struggling somewhat. It is difficult to observe him deteriorating.

I, too, have been facing some challenges. I was diagnosed with melanoma. I had surgery to remove it and have been receiving immunotherapy for the past several months. As a matter of fact, I have reviewed many stories while receiving treatments.

Currently, I am still working part time with our Special Task Force. Of late, I have been training a new officer. It has been very enjoyable and has generated some good stories. I will soon be turning it all over to him. Be looking for my next book that I intend to title *I Thought You Had Retired*.

As always, I thank my wonderful wife for her unending support. Most of all I thank the Lord above for sending His Son to die in my place. Choose Him. As I once again was reminded with Greg's tragic death, tomorrow isn't guaranteed.

God bless.

www.ingramcontent.com/pod-product-compliance
Lightning Source LLC
Chambersburg PA
CBHW071903290426
44110CB00013B/1265